WORLD WAR II

IN

500

PHOTOGRAPHS

TIME LIFE BOOKS

Editors Eileen Daspin, Michael Solomon
Consulting Designer Ryan Moore

Time Home Entertainment

Publisher Jim Childs
Vice President, Brand & Digital Strategy Steven Sandonato
Executive Director, Marketing Services Carol Pittard
Executive Director, Retail & Special Sales Tom Mifsud
Executive Publishing Director Joy Bomba
Director, Bookazine Development & Marketing Laura Adam
Vice President, Finance Vandana Patel
Publishing Director Megan Pearlman
Assistant General Counsel Simone Procas
Assistant Director, Special Sales Ilene Schreider
Senior Book Production Manager Susan Chodakiewicz
Brand Manager Katie McHugh Malm
Associate Prepress Manager Alex Voznesenskiy
Associate Project Manager Stephanie Braga

Editorial Director Stephen Koepp
Senior Editor Roe D'Angelo
Copy Chief Rina Bander
Design Manager Anne-Michelle Gallero
Editorial Operations Gina Scauzillo

SPECIAL THANKS
Katherine Barnet, Brad Beatson, Jeremy Biloon, Rose Cirrincione, Natalie
Ebel, Assu Etsubneh, Mariana Evans, Christine Font, Susan Hettleman,
Hillary Hirsch, David Kahn, Mona Li, Amy Mangus, Kimberly Marshall,
Nina Mistry, Dave Rozzelle, Ricardo Santiago, Adriana Tierno

Created by Contentra Technologies
Project Manager Phyllis Jelinek
Advisors Gordon Clarke, John Perritano
Designer Arvinder Kalsi
Photo Researcher Nivisha Sinha
Special Thanks Himanshu Chawla, Ritu Chopra, Md. Furqan, Ella Hanna,
Indrajeet Kumar, Prabhat Rastogi, Lisa Slone, and Sudhakar

ISBN-10: 1-60320-993-X
ISBN-13: 978-1-60320-993-9

We welcome your comments and suggestions about Time Home
Entertainment Books. Please write to us at:
Time Home Entertainment Books, Attention: Book Editors, P.O. Box 11016,
Des Moines, IA 50336-1016.
If you would like to order any of our hardcover Collector's Edition books,
please call us at 1-800-327-6388, Monday through Friday, 7 a.m.–8 p.m., or
Saturday, 7 a.m.–6 p.m., Central Time.

CONTENTS

The headline in the *New York Times* on September 1, 1939, captured the surprise in a crisp, bold headline: GERMAN ARMY ATTACKS POLAND; CITIES BOMBED, PORTS BLOCKADED.

That day, few understood that the invasion would spark the bloodiest war in human history—by the time the combat ended in 1945, almost 60 million people, civilian and military, lay dead.

In addition to those who died on the battlefield, millions more perished in concentration camps, on death marches, under the rubble of crushed cities, and from firestorms. Germany's Nazi government was particularly brutal, murdering six million Jews and others with factory-like precision. For its part, the United States bombed scores of enemy cities and dropped two nuclear weapons on Japan.

World War II in 500 Photographs covers this gripping narrative year by year, capturing cunning military strategy as it was conceived and behind-the-scenes political maneuvering and betrayals. It brings to life battles executed on land, sea, and in the air, and it sheds new light on the masterminds of war, exposing some of history's most infamous tyrants and its greatest heroes.

Photographs are at the heart of this book. As such, it is impossible to overstate the bravery of the photographers who chronicled the war from its beginning to the end. As you look at each image, keep in mind that the "shooters" often focused their cameras through the haze of bullets or antiaircraft fire. In addition to professionals, many soldiers also snapped their own photographs. Often these amateurs took pictures of their friends, their units, or local citizens in the area. Others recorded the horrors inflicted upon the elderly and children or a pile of dead enemy soldiers along a sunken road.

Each photograph is important in understanding the full scope of World War II. And each photographer is a witness. Walter Benjamin, a German Jew and noted philosopher who committed suicide in 1940 as the Nazis began their process of deportation and murder, asked if the photographer had the obligation of exposing the guilty with his photos.

Any good history book includes a lesson, and this book is no exception. Perhaps the greatest was articulated by British Prime Minister Winston Churchill in a May 8, 1945, speech: "I say that in the long years to come not only will the people of this island but of the world, wherever the bird of freedom chirps in human hearts, look back to what we've done and they will say 'do not despair, do not yield to violence and tyranny, march straightforward and die if need be—unconquered.'"

1 PRELUDE TO WAR

BY THE 1930S, EUROPE WAS ENGULFED IN THE GREAT DEPRESSION AND GERMANY WAS LOOKING FOR STRONG LEADERS TO SOLVE ITS POLITICAL AND ECONOMIC WOES.

"Today we rule Germany; tomorrow, the world."

—Adolf Hitler, 1938

Soldiers stood at attention during the Nazi Party rally of 1936 in Nuremberg, Germany. They were listening to a speech by the German Fuhrer, Adolf Hitler, delivered from the reviewing stand. The Nazis held a similar rally here every year between 1933 and 1938.

1919-1939

Change and Discontent

SOME HOPED THAT WORLD WAR I WOULD BE THE "WAR THAT ENDED ALL WARS."

A period of great upheaval swept over Europe after World War I. As centuries-old monarchies and empires collapsed, emergent states and new forms of government took their places. A global economic depression caused European economies to go from boom to bust. Post–World War I Europe was in shambles.

Hope ran high that the Treaty of Versailles, the pact ending war between the Allies and Germany, would provide a framework for peace. Each of the Allied leaders, however, had different goals. The British wanted money to pay for war damages, the French wanted to weaken Germany, and the United States wanted a lasting peace.

Failure at Versailles

The Treaty of Versailles, signed in 1919, marked the official end of the First World War. The so-called war guilt clause required Germany to accept responsibility "for causing all the loss and damage" to the Allies and their governments. Germany was also forced to relinquish control over territories it had taken, pay huge sums of money as reparations, and not rearm its military.

The terms of the treaty were a severe blow to German national pride and triggered economic hardship. The total cost of German reparations came to approximately $30 billion, the equivalent of about $2.7 trillion today. The German delegates to Versailles were outraged by the terms, but they were forced to sign the treaty and accept all its conditions, including the loss of their nation's overseas colonies. Over time, the pact provided immense propaganda value to national politicians like Adolf Hitler.

One idealistic provision of the treaty established the League of Nations, a global organization that would resolve international disputes to avert war. The terms, however, failed to provide the league with the ability to enforce its decisions, so the organization had little meaningful control over world events.

When the Nazis came to power, they ignored the provision of the accord forbidding Germany from rearming. The league and its member nations watched as Germany once again exerted its military prowess.

The March to War

Germany moved quickly toward extreme nationalism during the 1930s, culminating in the invasion of Poland in 1939.

Hitler began to rebuild German military.

JULY Nazi Party won a majority in the Reichstag, the German parliament.

▲ **JANUARY 30** Hitler was appointed chancellor of Germany.

MARCH "Enabling Act" was passed by the Reichstag, allowing Hitler's government to deviate from German constitution.

JUNE 30 Nazi "Night of the Long Knives" (see p. 10).

1930s • • • **1932** • • • • **1933** • • • • • **1934** • •

French Prime Minister George Clemenceau (left), American President Woodrow Wilson (center), and British Prime Minister Lloyd George (right) attended the Versailles Peace Conference in 1919.

Suffering from rapid inflation, Germans rushed to buy items at a department store in Berlin before prices could rise once again.

SEPTEMBER 15 Nuremberg Laws, which placed severe restrictions on Jews, were passed.

▲ **OCTOBER 3** Italy invaded Ethiopia, demonstrating the ineffectiveness of the League of Nations.

▲ **MARCH 7** Germany sent troops into Rhineland, violating the Treaty of Versailles.

OCTOBER 25 Rome-Berlin Axis was formed, linking the two fascist countries.

JULY Second Sino-Japanese War began.

MARCH 12–13 Germany annexed Austria.

▲ **SEPTEMBER 30** Czechs surrendered the Sudetenland to Germany.

SEPTEMBER 1 The war began when Germany invaded Poland.

1935 • 1936 • 1937 • 1938 • 1939

The Reichstag Fire

On the evening of February 27, 1933, the German parliament building, known as the Reichstag, burned. The Communist Party was falsely blamed for the arson, and the Nazis exploited the blaze to suspend freedom of speech, the press, and assembly.

By 1935, membership in the Nazi Party was virtually compulsory for children over the age of 10, and by 1940, the number of young people in the Hitler Youth organizations stood at about eight million.

Night of the Long Knives

The only possible threat to Hitler's leadership of the Nazis was the strength of the Sturmabteilung (SA), or "Brownshirts," that formed the paramilitary wing of the party. In June 1934, in an operation known as the Night of the Long Knives, Hitler had the leadership of the SA rounded up and killed. At Hitler's request, the Reichstag called the killings legal.

1919-1939

Hitler's Power Grab

GERMANY'S WEAK LEADERSHIP AND SEVERE ECONOMIC PROBLEMS LEAD TO THE RISE OF A DICTATOR.

Adolf Hitler was one of the founding members of the German Workers' Party, and in October 1919, he gave his first public speech to about 100 people. Within several months, he took over leadership of the party; by the end of 1920, it had been renamed the National Socialist German Workers' Party, or Nazi Party, and had several thousand members. Hitler used his skills at public speaking, coupled with intimidation from his street fighters, to rally others to his cause. In 1923, he was jailed for nine months, following an attempted overtaking of the government in the "Beer Hall Putsch." While in prison, Hitler wrote *Mein Kampf*, outlining his political ideology.

Notoriety from the putsch gave the Nazis a national presence. The party won 107 seats in the 1930 election. Two years later, it won 230 seats and became the largest party in the Reichstag. Then in January 1933, through legal means under the Weimar constitution, Hitler became chancellor of Germany. Within a year, he was a dictator.

In 1933, after some convoluted negotiations, German President Paul von Hindenburg appointed Adolf Hitler chancellor. Here, the two men shook hands.

Germany celebrated the annexation of Austria during the 1938 Reich Party Congress in Nuremberg. Here, Hitler returned the salute of the crowd. Rudolf Hess, deputy leader of the Nazi Party, was on the far left.

1919–1939

Japan and the Invasion of Manchuria

IN THE YEARS FOLLOWING WORLD WAR I, JAPAN BUILT ITSELF INTO A MAJOR MILITARY POWER.

Like other nations in the 1930s, Japan was hard hit by the Depression. Unemployment had soared in urban areas, and peasant farmers were facing starvation. At the same time, nationalist groups were looking for ways to expand access to raw materials to support the nation's growing industrial base. The northern Chinese province of Manchuria held a wealth of natural resources and some Japanese businesses already held investments in the region. Military officers believed it was time to invade and take the province. To create a pretext for an occupation, Japanese military officers in 1931 staged an explosion on a Japanese-owned railway in China, destroying a portion of the track. While the plan had not been authorized by Japan's government, military forces conquered the entire province and set up a puppet state. The League of Nations condemned the invasion but was powerless to take action.

Rape of Nanking

In December 1937, the Japanese army marched into the city of Nanking, China. Troops were issued an order to "kill all captives."

Over the course of the next six weeks, Japanese soldiers engaged in a horrific variety of war crimes. Between 250,000 and 300,000 civilians were murdered, tens of thousands of Chinese women—including the very young and the elderly—were raped. Shops and homes were looted, and one-third of the city was destroyed due to arson.

In 1931, thousands of Japanese troops were sent to occupy Manchuria.

In 1931, a rogue faction of the Japanese military bombed a railway station in Mukden, Manchuria, paving the way for the Japanese to invade China.

From Manchuria to Nanking

Japanese troops lined up behind a fortified wall near Mukden as they prepared for battle against the Chinese.

Kristallnacht

On November 9–10, 1938, paramilitary forces and non-Jewish civilians carried out a series of coordinated attacks on Jews, their homes, businesses, and synagogues throughout Nazi Germany. The event became known as Kristallnacht—or the "Night of Broken Glass"—in reference to the shattered windows that littered the streets.

1919-1939

The Rise of Fascism

FROM NATIONALISM TO DICTATORSHIPS

In 1919, Benito Mussolini organized World War I veterans and other Italians who were unhappy with the government. They called themselves the Fascist Party, a name meant to symbolize unity and authority, goals Mussolini had for himself and for Italy. During the next few years, Mussolini organized his supporters into the Blackshirts, squads of men who used violence to attain their objectives. In 1922,

Italian King Victor Emmanuel III, who feared civil war, asked Mussolini to serve as prime minister. By 1925, Mussolini had taken the title Il Duce, the leader, and had begun to suppress rival parties. He also curbed freedom of the press and replaced elected officials with members of his own party. While remaining a parliamentary monarchy in name, Italy had become a ruthless dictatorship that imprisoned or murdered its critics. The country's education system was revamped to promote fascism, and by the 1930s, Italy had developed a generation of young soldiers who were ready to serve their leader and expand Italy's power.

In the 1930s, Il Duce Benito Mussolini was celebrated as a strong leader who brought power and confidence to Italy. Here, Mussolini's bodyguards saluted him with knives raised.

Faces of War

"One of the men grabbed my father by the shoulder and spit in his face. They tore his World War I medals from his shirt and stomped them into the ground. They started beating my father. Furniture started flying through the windows. My mother was screaming: 'Let's get out of here. They are killing us.' We slipped out a back street, hoping the men would be finished soon and we could go back home."—Alex Lebenstein, eyewitness and survivor of Kristallnacht

2 | OUTBREAK OF WAR IN EUROPE

1939: BROKEN TREATIES AND ACTS OF GERMAN AGGRESSION TURNED EUROPE INTO A BATTLEFIELD, BUT THE UNITED STATES REMAINED NEUTRAL.

"Why should this war in the West be fought? For restoration of Poland? Poland of the Versailles Treaty will never rise again."

—Adolf Hitler, October 1939

Poles watched as the Luftwaffe flew over Warsaw. The outcome of the battle had already been decided.

1939

Germany Invades Czechoslovakia

HITLER DID NOT EXPECT BRITAIN OR FRANCE TO REACT WHEN HE BEGAN TO SEIZE NEW TERRITORY.

Though the Munich Pact of September 1938 ceded portions of Czechoslovakia to the Germans, Reich Chancellor Adolf Hitler was intent on annexing even more territory. As part of that plan, Germany entered into negotiations with the Czechs for control of the newly designated Sudetenland, a border region home to many German speakers.

Czechoslovakia's agreement, it turned out, was not needed. On March 14, 1939, Hitler contacted Czech president Emil Hácha to inform him that Germany was about to invade. The two met the following day, and Hácha was forced to "allow" the Germans to enter Bohemia and Moravia. As the Czech annexation unfolded, it became clear that the appeasement policies of the past decade were now ineffective.

The Nazi-Soviet Nonaggression Pact

Watching Czechoslovakia fall to the Nazis, Soviet Premier Joseph Stalin worried about Hitler's expansion eastward and a possible war with Germany. In the spring of 1939, the Soviet Union, France, and Britain held initial discussions about forming mutual assistance pacts designed to stem German aggression in eastern Europe.

Several months later, Stalin entered into talks with Hitler, who wanted to avoid fighting on two fronts. The two reached a nonaggression pact stipulating that their countries would not attack each other. In addition, Stalin agreed to allow Germany to invade Poland unopposed on the east, which both spared Russia a war on the eastern front and allowed the Soviets time to build up their military. The pact was signed on August 23.

On March 15, 1939, Hitler met with Czech President Emil Hácha in Berlin, where Hácha was told of the imminent German invasion.

Soviet Commissar of Foreign Affairs Vyacheslav Molotov (seated) signed the nonaggression pact with German Foreign Affairs Minister Joachim von Ribbentrop. The agreement divided eastern Europe into spheres of influence.

The Munich Pact

At the Munich Conference, Great Britain, France, Italy, and Germany signed an agreement that permitted Nazi Germany to annex parts of Czechoslovakia along the country's border with Germany. These portions of Czechoslovakia were home to a German-speaking population, who often felt the sting of prejudice in a foreign land. In an act to appease Hitler's demands—and to avoid another war—Britain and France accepted Hitler's request on the condition that he would never take another European territory. The agreement was signed on September 29, 1938, without Czechoslovakia's presence.

"Czechoslovakia has ceased to exist."
—Adolf Hitler, March 15, 1939

On September 29, 1938, Great Britain, France, and Italy accepted the transfer of the Czech Sudetenland to Germany. On October 1, 1938, Czechs showed both joy and sorrow as German troops entered the Sudetes.

Aggression Leads to War

Following decades of hostilities, World War II officially began in 1939.

1939
MAR

MARCH 15 Hitler invaded Czechoslovakia and claimed the territory for Germany.

MAY

MAY 22 Germany and Italy signed the Pact of Steel, forming the Axis powers.

AUG

AUGUST 23 The Soviet Union and Germany signed a non-aggression pact. Germany assumed it would not have to fight a war on two fronts.

SEPT

SEPTEMBER 1 German forces invaded Poland.
SEPTEMBER 3 Great Britain and France declared war on Germany.
SEPTEMBER 5 The United States affirmed its neutrality in the European war.
SEPTEMBER 17 The Soviet Union entered Poland from the east.
SEPTEMBER 27–29 Warsaw surrendered to Germany and the Soviet Union, which then divided Poland between them.

OCT

OCTOBER 8 Germans began to move Jews in Poland into Nazi-enforced ghettos, stripping them of their rights and restricting their movements.

DEC

DECEMBER 14 The Soviet Union was expelled from the League of Nations for aggression against Finland.

On September 1, 1939, Hitler addressed the Reichstag. He defended the invasion of Poland, claiming abuse of Germans who resided there.

1939

Germany Seizes Poland

HITLER ASSUMED THAT THE OTHER EUROPEAN NATIONS WOULD NOT INTERVENE WITH HIS EXPANSION PLANS.

Poland was next in Hitler's plan for territorial expansion, and the Poles sought to thwart a German attack by mobilizing their own troops in a show of force. The task, however, was daunting, as Poland had to defend itself from attack on three sides: Germany to the west, East Prussia to the north, and potentially Slovakia to the south. The government's only real option was to establish defensive lines along all the borders in question and to shore up protection of its major industrial centers.

To create a pretext for an invasion, German SS soldiers, clad in Polish army uniforms, crossed the border on August 31 and assaulted Germans living in the town of Gleiwitz. They left about a dozen dead inmates from German concentration camps, dressed in Polish army uniforms, as evidence of a Polish attack on German people.

The following day, on September 1, Hitler began the takeover of Poland. The German battleship *Schleswig-Holstein*, stationed in Gdansk Harbor, shelled a nearby Polish garrison. Minutes later, the Luftwaffe bombed Polish airfields, and about 1.5 million German soldiers quickly crossed into Poland. The German assault included about 2,000 tanks and more than 1,000 planes. The Polish army, using weapons that were largely obsolete, was unable to repel the superior German forces.

German soldiers passed through the Polish border in September.

German motorcycle units were used during the invasion. These troops were near the town of Bydgoszcz (Bromberg) in northern Poland.

Aboard his German bomber, this crew member was able to see Poland and one of its undamaged cities below.

With bombed-out buildings in the background, German soldiers prepared for a victory march in the newly occupied territory.

1939

On to Warsaw

HITLER'S FORCES SEIZED THE FORMER GERMAN
PROVINCES LOST TO POLAND AFTER WORLD WAR I.

Using newly developed blitzkrieg tactics, the German military quickly overran the first set of Polish defensive lines. Nazi aircraft then began battering Polish communications and supply centers to further weaken the nation. Within days, the Polish air force, severely damaged in the initial attacks, ran so low on fuel that it was virtually grounded.

German troops moved quickly through the country and began arriving at the outskirts of Warsaw between September 8 and 9. By late September, Warsaw was surrounded. No countries came to Poland's defense.

Blitzkrieg Warfare

Blitzkrieg warfare, or lightning war, was made possible by advances in technology developed between the two world wars. It stood in complete contrast to the stagnant trench battles of World War I. The tactics involved an initial rapid advancement of tank forces, supported by intense bombing from aircraft. The rapid two-pronged strategy allowed aggressors to surround defending troops. Those soldiers could then be eliminated, and the invading army could follow behind the advancement. Wireless radio provided a means for tanks, aircraft, and mobile infantry to communicate and coordinate these rapid attacks. Blitzkrieg attacks were especially successful against nations like Poland, that could mount only a thin front line and had few places to retreat.

By October 1, 1939, German
motorcycle troops openly patrolled
the streets of occupied Warsaw.

Citizens of Warsaw ran for shelter as the Luftwaffe poured incendiary bombs down on the city.

This photograph of devastated buildings helped document the brutality of the German war machine.

A German heavy gun stood in position, ready to fire on Warsaw. More than 80 percent of the city was destroyed during the bombing.

Homes and other bombed-out buildings revealed the effects of the Warsaw siege. Germany's use of heavy guns and mortars resulted in heavy civilian losses.

1939

A City Under Siege

POLISH FORCES DEFENDING WARSAW
WERE STRONG, BUT THEY WERE
OVERWHELMED BY THE NAZI INVADERS.

To avoid a protracted battle for Warsaw, Germany first surrounded the city with well-armed troops, then bombed it from a relatively safe distance. Utilities, hospitals, and markets, as well as the expected military targets, were quickly destroyed.

Some soldiers retreating from the fighting at Bzura, west of Warsaw, joined the remaining Polish troops trying to defend Warsaw and the nearby city Modlin. But by September 22, the German siege was in full force, and all communications outside the two cities were cut off. Warsaw was shelled around the clock for several days in preparation for the final assault. While Polish military forces had some supplies and could hold out for a bit longer, the civilian population of Warsaw suffered tremendously. The German army had instructions that no civilians were to be allowed to leave the city. Following the destruction of water systems, there was no potable water available anywhere in the city and food was impossible to come by.

On September 26, the German 8th Army attacked the city from the south with heavy air and artillery bombing. Communications within Warsaw were destroyed, and there was no electric power. The German 3rd Army followed up with an artillery barrage from the north. When Polish envoys asked for a cease-fire, the request was refused, and the Germans indicated that they would only accept an unconditional surrender.

On September 27, 1939, Warsaw surrendered to the Germans. The following day, the city of Modlin, which was under assault by both the German 3rd and 8th Armies, capitulated. Twenty-four thousand exhausted Polish troops surrendered.

Homeless and destitute, Polish refugees tried to care for their children. The propaganda poster in the background reads, "To arms—United, we will defeat the enemy!"

1939

The USSR Marches on Poland

STALIN'S FORCES IMPOSED THEIR OWN IDEOLOGY
ON LOCAL CITIZENS AND CRUSHED OBJECTORS.

Hitler was not the only leader seeking to annex Poland. As the Germans swept across the country from the west, Stalin concluded it was time for the Red Army to invade from the east. At 3:00 a.m. on September 17, the Polish ambassador in Moscow received a note that said that the Soviet government had ordered the high command of the Red Army to send its troops across the frontier to take under their protection the lives and welfare of the populations of western Ukraine and western Belorussia.

Within hours, the Soviet Union had mounted its own brutal invasion. Determined that Poland would not regain its independence, the Soviets began eliminating those it considered to be potential threats. Polish military officers were shipped to camps in Russia, and the remaining leaders and thinkers were incarcerated. Many were executed.

On September 17, 1939, a column of Soviet armored vehicles approached the Polish border. Polish forces had hoped for British and French support but met Soviet invaders instead.

Soldiers of the Red Army vastly outnumbered Polish forces and captured more than 200,000, who became prisoners of war.

While von Ribbentrop and Soviet Premier Joseph Stalin watched, Molotov checked the plans for the demarcation of Poland.

1939

The USSR and Germany Divide Poland

WHILE THEIR POLICIES DIFFERED, SOVIETS AND GERMANS PROVED EQUALLY HOSTILE TO THE POLISH POPULATION, KILLING NEARLY SIX MILLION PEOPLE.

By fall 1939, the occupation of Poland by Germany and the Soviet Union was complete. The country was divided along the Bug River, and Germany had acquired territories along the eastern border. In Soviet-occupied territory, elections were staged to formalize the annexation. State-owned properties and businesses were nationalized and collectivized. Those who had served in the Polish military were taken prisoner and sent to camps outside the country.

In the German-occupied territory, western Poland was incorporated into Germany. Roughly one million Poles were expelled to the east and at the same time, Germans were brought in to settle the newly annexed territory. The division of Poland would hold until May 1945.

On October 6, Hitler gave a speech in the Reichstag defending the military actions. He argued that the conquests of Czechoslovakia and Poland were done to right the wrongs of the Treaty of Versailles and that he had offered a peace proposal to Britain and France. Hitler claimed that he had no desire to go to war against France and Britain, even though they had declared war against his country. He noted that Britain and France had rejected his offers for peace negotiations.

German and Soviet troops participated in a ceremony held at Brest-Litovsk, marking the Polish demarcation.

German soldiers conversed with a Russian tank crew stationed in Poland.

Soviet and German leaders gathered to study maps of Poland. While many civilians initially favored the Soviet occupation, their support faded as Soviet repression became part of daily life.

Division of Poland

Following negotiations between Russia and Germany, new borders were drawn for Polish territory.

In October 1939, German soldiers, who were searching for hidden weapons, began arresting Jews in Warsaw.

1939

Ghettos in Poland

JEWS IN POLAND HAD BEEN MISTREATED AND ISOLATED, AND THE COUNTRY BECAME THE DESTINATION FOR JEWS FROM OTHER GERMAN-OCCUPIED TERRITORIES.

On October 8, two days after the end of formal fighting in Poland, the Germans began moving the country's Jewish population, about two million people, into ghettos. The Nazis sealed the country's borders so Jews could not escape, and the ghettos in larger cities were barricaded with walls and barbed wire fences. These areas served as large prison camps, with entrances guarded by German police or SS troops. The largest ghetto was in Warsaw, where more than 350,000 Jews were confined to an area of 1.3 square miles and subjected to strict curfews. Jews were forced to live in appalling conditions, treated as "undesirables," stripped of their culture and eventually, of their humanity.

Concentrating the Jewish population into small areas made mass deportations simple for the Nazis. Between July and September 1942, over 300,000 of the Jews in the Warsaw ghetto were removed and sent to Treblinka, where most were immediately killed. In addition to the deportations, dozens of slave labor camps were built, and Jewish males were assigned to forced, brutal labor details.

In Zydom, Poland, three German soldiers watched as a civilian shaved an Orthodox Jew, an act of humiliation.

Nazi SS troops herded Jews into lines before sending them to concentration camps. Many died on the journey, and many more died in the camps.

1939

The Soviet Union Invades Finland

PROTECTING THEIR HOMELAND, THE FINNS PROVED TO BE STRONGER THAN THE RED ARMY HAD EVER EXPECTED.

The Soviet Union was concerned that Finland, a mere 20 miles from Leningrad, would be the Germans' next target and soon fall into Nazi hands. The Russians, too, had designs on Finland, whose northernmost territory overlooked Murmansk, a strategic seaport that Russia was anxious to maintain. In an effort to protect Murmansk, the Soviet Union offered Finland a land exchange. If the Finns would give up the northern lands near the port and Leningrad, the Russians would give them territory more to the south in Karelia.

The Finns met with the Russians in mid-October and after several weeks of deliberations, refused the deal. The Soviet response was swift. On November 30, Stalin deployed about 450,000 troops in an invasion. The move prompted the League of Nations to expel the Soviet Union and to rally other nations behind Finland. Denmark, Sweden, and Norway reaffirmed their neutrality in the conflict.

In late December 1939, the Finns launched a counterattack in the West and destroyed two Soviet divisions. The war lasted 105 days. While the Finns lost some territory, they were able to prevent a Soviet takeover. By the end of the winter, both sides were exhausted and agreed to sign the Moscow Peace Treaty in March 1940 to end the conflict. The accord granted the Soviet Union some Finnish territory, but it preserved Finland's independence and ended Soviet attempts to annex the country.

Finnish machine-gun crews blended in with the environment. The Finns lacked war matériel and often resorted to taking ammunition from fallen Russians.

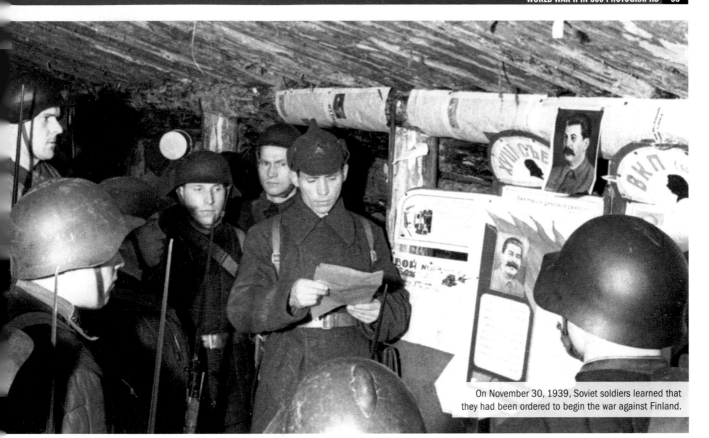

On November 30, 1939, Soviet soldiers learned that they had been ordered to begin the war against Finland.

Finnish "ghost troops" were skilled in cross-country skiing and were accustomed to the harsh weather conditions, which they used to their advantage.

1939

Declarations of War by Britain and France

PRIME MINISTER NEVILLE CHAMBERLAIN GREETED THE WAR WITH PROFOUND DISAPPOINTMENT. THE LONG STRUGGLE TO WIN PEACE HAD FAILED.

Just two days after the Nazi invasion of Poland on September 1, Britain, France, Australia, and New Zealand declared war on Germany. South Africa and Canada followed a few days later.

On the evening of September 3, 1939, Britain dropped 13 tons of leaflets over Germany telling citizens that their rulers had condemned them to the massacres, miseries, and privations of a war they could not ever hope to win. That same night, a German submarine U-30 torpedoed the British passenger liner *Athenia*, killing 112.

Of all the Allies, France, which had been building up its troops and supplies throughout the 1930s, was the only country prepared to directly attack Germany. With aid from the British, French troops advanced on the German defenses along the border between the two countries. Following the collapse of Poland, Germany was able to divert troops to the French border and push the French back to the Maginot Line, the defensive barricade between France and Germany built in the 1930s. In the following months, there was scant activity on the French front. In fact, things were so quiet there, some derided the battles and called it "The Phony War." Even in Germany, it was called the "Sitzkrieg," the sitting war.

Many nations, including the U.S., remained neutral. The Belgians and Dutch barred British and French soldiers from their soil and remained neutral. Despite these actions, both countries were invaded on May 10, 1940.

Crowds looked up at Big Ben in London on September 3, when Britain's ultimatum to Germany expired. Unless Germany ceased hostilities and withdrew from Poland, Britain and France promised to go to war. Germany did not respond.

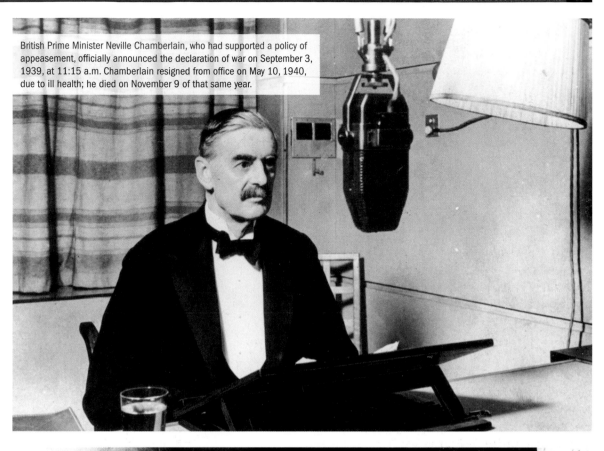

British Prime Minister Neville Chamberlain, who had supported a policy of appeasement, officially announced the declaration of war on September 3, 1939, at 11:15 a.m. Chamberlain resigned from office on May 10, 1940, due to ill health; he died on November 9 of that same year.

The British declaration of war was read from the steps of London's Royal Exchange. Soon after, air-raid sirens sounded across the city, but it was a false alarm.

In 1939, sheets of corrugated steel were distributed to London residents so that they could make their own air-raid shelters.

The Anderson Shelter

The Anderson shelter, made from sheets of corrugated steel and then covered by soil, was a type of air-raid defense used in Britain. Because these structures were usually installed in the garden, people would often plant flowers, fruits, and vegetables in the soil roofs to make them more attractive and useful. Anderson shelters could hold up to six people and performed well in the bombing raids.

1939

German Air Raids on Britain

ATTACKS FROM THE SKY STARTED IN THE FALL OF 1939, AND THEY BECAME ALL TOO FREQUENT.

The first German air attack on Britain took place just six weeks into the war. On October 16, 1939, a group of nine German bomber aircraft damaged three ships: the destroyer HMS *Southampton* and two cruisers, the HMS *Mohawk* and HMS *Edinburgh.*

During the assault, the British scrambled Spitfire fighter planes to intercept the Germans and managed to shoot down several Nazi aircraft.

On October 28, another air battle took place, this time over East Lothian in Scotland. During that skirmish, a German airplane was shot down and captured, intact, on British soil. As German airpower grew, these small incursions would set the stage for much larger confrontations to come.

A group of British citizens surveyed the street from a communal shelter.

German Junkers prepared for battle in 1939. While these "Wunderbombers" were fast and versatile, they were vulnerable to the faster British Spitfires.

Following Britain's declaration of war, President Franklin Roosevelt addressed the United States, appealing for neutrality.

1939

The United States Debates Entering the War

PUBLICLY, PRESIDENT ROOSEVELT SWORE TO THE AMERICAN PEOPLE THAT THE U.S. WOULD NOT ENTER THE WAR UNLESS ATTACKED. PRIVATELY, HE PREPARED THE NATION FOR BATTLE.

In 1939, many Americans supported Britain and France but wanted to stay out of what was viewed as a European war. President Franklin D. Roosevelt expressed a similar opinion in a fireside chat delivered to the nation on September 3. Legally, the U.S. was prevented from intervening because of the American Neutrality Act of 1935, which made no distinction between the aggressor and the victim. Hitler, too, wanted to keep the U.S. out of the war and ordered German naval forces to go to great lengths not to provoke America.

Yet this dynamic changed once Germany invaded Poland. Some Americans began to question aspects of the Neutrality Act, and on September 21, 1939, Roosevelt called for a special session of Congress to try to repeal some portions of law, including the embargo against sending military aid to other countries. By early November, Congress had amended the Neutrality Act to allow arms and matériel to be supplied to Britain and France under certain conditions. Both countries would be permitted to buy war matériel from the U.S., but they would be required to pay for them in cash, and they had to pick up the items themselves. This was known as the "cash and carry" plan. The arrangement addressed the concerns of some that loans or credit purchases would not be repaid—a problem faced after World War I. Roosevelt continued to push for all aid short of war and agreed to trade 50 U.S. warships for eight British military bases.

> **"When peace has been broken anywhere, the peace of all countries everywhere is in danger."**
>
> —Franklin D. Roosevelt

This World War II factory in Stratford, Connecticut, produced over 6,000 Corsairs—fighter planes with fold-up wings that could be used aboard aircraft carriers. Wartime manufacturing boosted the American economy, which had been suffering for more than a decade following the Great Depression.

3 | WAR ACROSS TWO CONTINENTS

1940: THE EVENTS OF 1940 PROVED THAT THE CONFLICT IN EUROPE WAS NO "PHONY WAR," AS GERMANY AND ITALY INVADED NATION AFTER NATION ACROSS TWO CONTINENTS.

By May 1940, German troops marched unopposed through towns, large and small, in the Netherlands. The occupation lasted five years, and the toll on human life was enormous.

"Like so many of our people, we have now had a personal experience of German barbarity which only strengthens the resolve of all of us to fight through to final victory."

—King George VI of Britain, September 1940

1940

A Scandinavian Offensive

THE NAZIS CONQUERED DENMARK IN JUST SIX HOURS
BUT MET UNEXPECTED RESISTANCE IN NORWAY.

In 1940, Germany's military leaders developed plans to simultaneously invade Norway and Denmark for different strategic motives. Norway was key for its ports, which the Nazis wanted for shipping and receiving raw materials, while Denmark would provide an excellent staging position for German aircraft to repel possible attacks from Britain.

In one of the swiftest takeovers of a country ever recorded, the Nazis invaded Denmark first, in the predawn hours of April 9, 1940. The Danish air force was virtually wiped out before its second plane left the ground, and the seriously overmatched and outnumbered Danish military could do little to defend the nation. Denmark surrendered six hours after the initial attack.

German troops patrolled the streets of Copenhagen in May. Danish law enforcement was forced to cooperate with Nazi occupiers.

More Nations Join the War

Some countries that sought to remain neutral and stay out of the war were targeted for invasion by Germany and Italy.

FEBRUARY 15 Hitler ordered unrestricted submarine warfare.

MARCH 12 Finland signed a peace treaty with the Soviet Union.

▲ **MARCH 19** British planes dropped the first bombs on German soil.

APRIL 9 Germany invaded Denmark and Norway. Denmark surrendered the same day.

1940   **FEBRUARY**   •   •   •   •   **MARCH**   •   •   •   **APRIL**   •   •   •

By May, German antitank units had erected camouflaged positions amid Denmark's coastal sand dunes.

▲ **MAY 10** Germany invaded Belgium, the Netherlands, and Luxembourg. Winston Churchill became British prime minister.

MAY 12 German forces crossed into France.

MAY 25 Allied forces retreated to Dunkirk.

JUNE 11 Italy declared war on the Allies.

▲ **JUNE 14** Germans entered Paris.

JUNE 25 France surrendered to Germany.

JULY 10 Battle of Britain, the first major campaign to be fought entirely by air forces, began.

SEPTEMBER 7 London Blitz began.

▲ **SEPTEMBER 27** Germany, Italy, and Japan signed the Tripartite Pact.

MAY • • • • **JUNE** • • • • **JULY** • • • • **SEPTEMBER**

German troops set up their big guns on one of the many battlefronts in Norway. The Nazis attacked by sea and air before sending in ground troops.

1940

A Battle for Norway's Waterways

WITH BRITISH AND FRENCH SUPPORT, THE NORWEGIANS
KEPT THE NAZIS AT BAY FOR TWO MONTHS.

With Denmark having surrendered at about 6:00 a.m. on April 9, the Germans dispatched warships loaded with weapons and troops into Norway to seize their primary target: the ports and coastal waterways of Norway that were needed for shipping and for transporting iron ore. There had been talk of the Allies potentially sending troops to occupy the Scandinavian nation, which was neutral at the time, and the Germans wanted to guarantee that

ships ferrying the ore south could continue uninterrupted.

Narvik, a town located on a fjord along the northwest coast of Norway, was considered particularly important to this mission, dubbed Operation *Weserübung*. During the winter months when rail travel was more challenging, the ore could be moved over waters from Sweden to Narvik, then down the western coast of Norway and finally into Germany. For the Germans, Narvik would also serve as a valuable naval base.

The Assault

Unlike the Danish forces, the Norwegian military was able to resist the German onslaught, at least initially, buying time for the Norwegian royal family and the country's government to escape to Britain.

Two months after the invasion began, the Norwegians surrendered and Germany began its occupation of the country. A Nazi-friendly government was installed, and police forces were controlled by the Nazis. The occupation lasted until 1945.

Heavily armed German infantrymen marched into Norway. Troops expected little resistance and were ordered to fire only if fired upon.

German soldiers were on patrol and ready to attack during the April invasion of Norway.

1940

Germany Targets the Netherlands

HITLER HAD PROMISED NOT TO DRAW THE DUTCH INTO THE WAR. AS
WITH SO MANY OTHER VOWS, HE HAD NO INTENTION OF HONORING IT.

Like many other European nations, the Netherlands had hoped to remain neutral during the war. Initially, Germany considered respecting the country's wishes; however, it quickly decided that Dutch airfields would be valuable in a later fight against Britain, and that the Allies might think the same in their battle against Germany.

On May 10, 1940, a month after the successful invasions of Norway and Denmark, the Germans marched into the Netherlands, expecting to capture the country quickly. The Luftwaffe dropped paratroopers over Dutch airfields and secured bridges and other strategic points well before the invading ground forces arrived—and well before Allied forces could come to the aid of the Dutch. The city of Rotterdam surrendered on May 14 after being massively bombarded by the Luftwaffe, and the rest of the country surrendered the following day.

The Dutch royal family managed to escape to Britain, but the Netherlands remained occupied by Germany until the final days of the war.

German soldiers crossed the River Meuse at Maastricht on May 11, as they headed south to Belgium. Maastricht, a vital traffic hub, had surrendered the day before.

While the Dutch watched with shock and disbelief, German military paraded through Amsterdam on a route that took them past the queen's palace.

1940

South to Belgium

FRENCH AND BRITISH TROOPS WHO
ARRIVED TO SAVE THE DAY WERE INSTEAD
SURROUNDED BY THE GERMANS.

Germany was on a march, virtually unopposed throughout Europe. On the same day the Nazis invaded the Netherlands, they also began their attack on Belgium and Luxembourg. Smaller than Rhode Island and with scant defenses, Luxembourg was easy prey for the Germans and fell within the day. Belgium, which was better armed and had the help of French and British troops, put up a stronger fight.

The initial German assault on Belgium came directly from the east. The Germans employed gliders to deliver men and explosives to strategic locations. Belgian troops and pilots fought to slow the Germans as much as possible until the Allies could come to their rescue. When the French and British armies finally arrived to help repel the German advance, they were drawn into the center of the country. Their attempt to repel the Germans proved futile. A second German thrust from the southeast through the Ardennes effectively encircled the Allies, who were then caught in a pocket along the English Channel.

German soldiers took shelter behind a low wall in a Belgian town in May 1940. Like the other countries that had declared neutrality, Belgium was outmanned.

German Panzer III tanks plowed through Flanders, in northern Belgium. The first tank battle of the war, the Battle of Hannut, took place during this invasion.

When the Germans invaded Belgium, about two million civilians panicked and left their homes. Here, a family escaped the town of Louvain, which was destroyed by bombing.

Members of the Royal Ulster Rifles waited on an improvised pier of trucks during the evacuation. An estimated 198,000 British and 140,000 French soldiers were saved during Operation Dynamo.

Thousands of Allied troops lined the beach at Dunkirk, waiting to be rescued.

1940

Operation Dynamo: The Evacuation of Dunkirk

PRIME MINISTER WINSTON CHURCHILL HAILED THE RETREAT AS A "MIRACLE OF DELIVERANCE" BUT WARNED THAT WARS WOULD NOT BE WON BY WITHDRAWING.

The Germans forced the Allied troops who had been defending Belgium to move south and then trapped them along the northern coast of France. Isolated at Dunkirk, the only port along the English Channel available for evacuation, the troops needed to get out. The French First Army battled hard to stall the Germans while the British prepared an emergency evacuation named Operation Dynamo. A makeshift fleet of watercraft ranging from destroyers to pleasure boats were called to duty, and within nine days, more than 330,000 British, Belgian, and French troops were rescued from the shores of Dunkirk, just six miles south of the Belgian border.

The withdrawal concluded on June 4, 1940. Allied forces left behind tanks, artillery, and heavy equipment. More importantly, they ceded control of Belgium and northern France to the Germans.

A Fatal Error
Reichsmarschall Hermann Göring had assured Hitler that the Luftwaffe could decimate the Allies. When German army forces had to move in, they met unexpected resistance. Hitler called off the attack and chose not to pursue the Allies, a move that allowed them to evacuate from Dunkirk. This tactical error has been called a turning point of the war.

1940

The Fall of France

THE NAZIS' SWIFT VICTORY RUINED BRITAIN'S
STRATEGY FOR FIGHTING HITLER IN EUROPE.

In the 1930s, France built the Maginot Line, a barrier of concrete forts, obstacles, and weapons along its border with Germany, to defend itself from another invasion. While formidable, the fortifications were designed for World War I tactics and only protected one border. Ultimately, the Maginot Line was insufficiently manned, and Germany just went around it. The well-armed German army in northern France continued its push south.

France had a powerful army, and its soldiers fought well. Still, without the men who had been evacuated from Dunkirk, the French were vastly outnumbered by their historic foe. German tanks and troops were able to push quickly on to Paris, arriving on June 14, the day after the French government had fled south to the city of Bordeaux. Thousands of Parisians had already escaped from the city. After a short period of chaos, France signed an armistice with Germany. Reich Chancellor Adolf Hitler's forces were given control of the north and west of the country. A nominally separate government was tasked to lead the "*zone libre*" unoccupied portion of the country. The agreement was signed on June 22, less than two months after the battle of France began. The document of capitulation was made even more humiliating for the French because Hitler insisted that it be signed in the same railway car used when Germany surrendered at the close of World War I.

Allied soldiers did not give up France without a fight. Beginning June 5, the Germans engaged them in fierce battles.

A piece of heavy artillery camouflaged by netting was loaded during action on the French front.

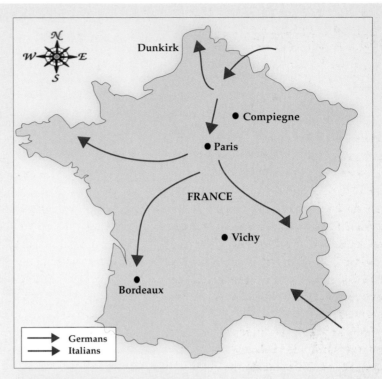

Invasion from the North and South

While German troops invaded France from the north, Italians came in from the southeastern border.

French soldiers transported supplies along the Maginot Line.

French Premier Philippe Pétain saluted troops during a military review while Vice Premier Pierre Laval (right) and other Vichy officials watched.

English Channel

GERMANY

•Paris

FRANCE

Bay of Biscay

Vichy •

Lyon•

ITALY

Bordeaux•

Marseille
•

Mediterranean Sea

Occupied Zone
"Free" Zone

"It is with heavy heart that I tell you today we must stop fighting."

—Philippe Pétain

Vichy France

Following the signing of the armistice agreement, the French government resigned and a new government, headquartered in the city of Vichy and under the leadership of Philippe Pétain, was formed. Formally called the French State, Vichy France lay in the southeastern part of the country and controlled about two-fifths of France. The French slogan "Liberty, Equality, Fraternity" was replaced with a new one: "Work, Family, Fatherland." This so-called legitimate government was authoritarian and collaborated openly with the Nazis. The Vichy government lasted until September 1944, when Paris was liberated.

In an influential speech delivered from the BBC in London on June 18, General Charles de Gaulle urged the French people to resist the Nazis and to continue the fight.

"France has lost a battle. But France has not lost the war."

—Charles de Gaulle

Charles de Gaulle: Leader in Exile

When German forces invaded France in early May 1940, General Charles de Gaulle had been leading a tank brigade. An ardent nationalist, he flew to England, and on June 28, the British recognized him as the leader of the Free French. De Gaulle broadcast messages to his countrymen, urging resistance against the Germans and against the Vichy government. De Gaulle's influence was minor at first, but he rapidly gained a following among expatriate French military personnel.

From his post in London, de Gaulle organized troops in the French colonies to fight with their Allied colleagues. French colonies in Africa rallied to support the Free French, and later in the war, these forces joined the Allies on the battlefield.

A volunteer civilian aircraft spotter watched the skies from the roof of a building near St. Paul's Cathedral in London.

1940

The Battle of Britain: The Finest Hour

WHEN THE LUFTWAFFE FAILED TO DOMINATE IN THE AIR, HITLER
AND HIS MILITARY LEADERS WERE FORCED TO CHANGE STRATEGIES.

Once France fell to the Nazis, it became apparent that the Germans' next target would be Great Britain. Using tactics that had worked in the past, Hitler sought to use the Luftwaffe to destroy the Royal Air Force. He believed this strategy would force Britain to come to terms that would end the war. Hitler also began making plans to invade the island nation.

The Battle of Britain began in July with assaults on English convoys and ports. The attacks broadened and intensified; new targets included radar stations and airplane factories. The German bombing caused extensive damage, both physically and psychologically, and the country knew it could not sustain such deep losses for an extended period of time. However, the RAF was resilient and German aircraft were operating at the extreme limit of their range. By August, 600 Luftwaffe planes had been downed, while the British had lost 260.

Even as the German air attacks continued, the failure of the Luftwaffe to dominate proved a turning point in the war. Hitler and his military leaders eventually gave up on plans to invade Britain. The battle plan evolved and changed direction as the Germans decided to focus on the sea and on blockading British ports.

A formation of Hawker Hurricanes, as well as Spitfires, battled in the air against the Germans.

Firestorms that resulted from the bombings blazed through London.

Two German bombers flew over the Silvertown area of London's Docklands, the site of one of the largest gas works in Europe.

Business as Usual

The Blitz, while horrific, failed to destroy the spirit of the British people. Many cities were bombed during these months, but it was London that bore the brunt of the attacks. Over a million homes were destroyed and thousands of people were killed. Amid the destruction, the British pressed on with their lives, trying to maintain a sense of normality and determined not to let Hitler get the best of them. It was "business as usual."

1940

The Blitz

HOPING TO INSTILL FEAR AND BOMB BRITAIN INTO SUBMISSION, THE GERMANS CONDUCTED DEADLY NIGHTTIME RAIDS.

On August 24, a German plane on its way to a military target drifted off course and accidentally dropped a bomb in the center of London. The following night, in retaliation, British planes made a bombing run over Berlin. Property damage was minimal, but Germans were stunned. In the weeks that followed, Britain followed up with several more aerial assaults on Berlin. These strikes provoked a change in German military strategy. From that point on, German bombers attacked British military, industrial, and civilian targets alike, including large British cities.

The campaign dubbed the Blitz began on September 7, 1940. On that afternoon, Germany sent about 350 bombers and 600 fighters to pound London. Several hours later, a second group of planes unleashed a new wave of destruction. London was hit 57 nights in a row. Other large cities suffered as well. One November night in Coventry, German planes dropped incendiary bombs that destroyed some 50,000 buildings including a good number of the city's factories, killing more than 500 and injuring around 1,000. The Blitz lasted eight months, well into 1941.

During a German air raid on October 14, a bomb exploded on Balham High Street, London. The next morning, a public bus tumbled into the crater.

Families fled their homes and camped out in Tube stations when they heard the air-raid sirens.

The Underground

At the beginning of the Blitz, the government feared that people would take refuge from night air raids in the London Underground and closed the subway line to the public. Yet once it was shown that Tube stations were effective shelters against explosives and incendiary bombs, officials reopened the Tube, allowing about 170,000 people to routinely take shelter there each evening.

1940

Operation Pied Piper

NEARLY THREE MILLION BRITISH, MOSTLY CHILDREN, WERE EVACUATED FROM THEIR HOMES.

The British had expected that a blitzkrieg attack would come from Germany, even if they did not know exactly when. To remove the more vulnerable citizens from harm's way, the British began Operation Pied Piper. Children and the elderly were evacuated from London and other cities to safer locations in rural England and overseas to other countries in the Commonwealth.

Later, when it was believed that there might be an actual invasion, the evacuees who had been transported to the south and east of Britain were again moved away from anticipated fighting.

Thousands of children were removed from London. Labeled like luggage, children said good-bye to their parents and were herded onto trains.

Thousands of children were sent from London to England's western counties. For many, it seemed as if they were going on an adventure or a holiday.

Signs provided evacuation schedules. The exodus worked well, but at times there were problems with housing and food once children reached their new homes.

WE SELL
SOLIDOX
TOOTHPASTE

GOVERNMENT

EVACUATION

SCHEME

School Children from this area
can now be evacuated

REGISTER AT
The following Schools
    Chelsham (C. of E.)
    Brockley Central Girls (Oxted)
    Limpsfield Chart, Infants
    Limpsfield (C. of E.)
    Merle Common (Council)
    Oxted (County)
    Oxted (C. of E.)
    Tatsfield
on
FRIDAY, 7th July, 9 a.m. - 4 p.m.
SATURDAY, 8th JULY, 9 a.m. - 12 noon

On September 8, 1940, Arab cavalrymen working with Italian forces charged on military positions in British Somaliland. British forces soon left the African colony.

Britain's Western Desert Force attacked Sidi Barrani, Egypt, on December 9. Days later, Italian prisoners were forcibly removed from the town. By January 1941, the British had driven the Italian 10th Army from Egypt.

1940
Italy Lands in North Africa

ITALIAN FORCES OUTNUMBERED THE BRITISH IN LIBYA AND EGYPT,
BUT THE BRITISH WERE BETTER EQUIPPED, TRAINED, AND LED.

Benito Mussolini, Italy's leader, saw the vast amount of land gained by Germany and Russia, and he intended to increase Italy's holdings as well. Mussolini looked across the Mediterranean Sea to Africa and made his move. In early August 1940, while Germany was beginning its battle over the skies of Britain, Italian troops in East Africa crossed into British Somaliland. The outnumbered British troops fought back, but they were forced to withdraw. By the end of August, the Italians occupied the country.

Italy's successful action in East Africa was followed by another foray, this time in North Africa. In September, Italian forces in Libya launched an invasion of Egypt. Their goal was to capture the Suez Canal. The Italian advance stalled three days later. Italy's forces had begun their initial attack on Greece on October 28, 1940, and, as a result, the campaign in Egypt became a low priority. British and Indian forces counterattacked in early December, and by the end of the month, the Italians were forced to withdraw from Egypt.

The Suez Canal
The war in North Africa was fought largely over control of the Suez Canal. Completed in 1869, this man-made waterway connected the Mediterranean with the Red Sea, which made ship transport between Europe and Asia possible without having to go entirely around Africa. Britain had installed a significant military force to protect the canal and its access to Middle Eastern oil and Asian raw materials. The Suez Canal was a highly coveted prize, and hence, a prime target.

Scottish Cameron Highlander and Indian troops marched past the pyramids at Giza as they prepared to defend against the advancing Italians.

1940

Rommel Deployed

THE BOLD ACTIONS OF GERMANY'S AFRIKA KORPS COMMANDER WOULD SURPRISE HIS ENEMIES.

After a series of devastating defeats in Africa in late 1940, the Italians requested assistance from Germany. In response, Hitler formed the Afrika Korps, whose mission was to help his ally retain the territory it had taken in North Africa. Hitler selected Commander Erwin Rommel to lead this new force. As commander of a Panzer division during the Battle of France, Rommel had gained fame for the speed and surprise of his attacks.

The Afrika Korps arrived in Libya in February 1941 and quickly began to win battles, turning the tides of war in North Africa in favor of the Axis powers. Rommel had been ordered to hold the Allies where they were, but by the end of April 1941, the German commander had pushed Allied forces east, back to the Egyptian border.

Nazi Policy in North Africa

Far from the concentration camps of Nazi-occupied Europe, the Jewish population of Africa suffered a less-gruesome fate than their peers to the north. While the Nazis did occupy Tunisia for a short time, they lacked the resources and the time to devise an efficient system of genocide. However, the Jews of North Africa were still subjected to acts of antisemitism, often stripped of their property by both the local European population and the native Muslims. After the French armistice with Germany was signed in 1940, the Vichy government sent Jewish refugees from Europe to forced labor camps in Morocco and Algeria. Local Jews attempted to intervene on their behalf, trying to get them visas to the United States. When the Nazis invaded and occupied Tunisia, they arrested and persecuted many Jewish leaders and sent many more to detention camps.

British infantry used trenches abandoned by Italian troops in Egypt. In December, the 4th Armoured Brigade took the fort at Sidi Omar, along with nearly 1,000 Italian prisoners.

Members of the Jewish community in Tunisia volunteered to serve with the Free French troops in North Africa.

1940

A Bungled Invasion

ITALY UNDERESTIMATED THE GREEKS AND WAS
QUICKLY FORCED TO RETREAT TO ALBANIA.

The Greeks reacted furiously when Mussolini, seeking to assert an Italian presence in the Balkans, demanded to occupy their country. Dictator Ioannis Metaxas rejected Il Duce's ultimatum, and when Italian forces crossed eastward through Albania on October 28, Metaxas dispatched a highly motivated Greek army.

Taking advantage of mountainous terrain they knew well, the Greek troops easily outmaneuvered the Italians and pushed them back into Albania within two weeks. By mid-December, the Greeks occupied nearly a quarter of Albania, tying up over half a million Italian troops.

Mussolini had not informed Hitler of his plans to invade, and Hitler denounced the action as a blunder. He had hoped that the Italians would focus their energy on the North African campaign. Instead, the conflict in Greece reached a stalemate that would last into the coming year.

In November, shortly after the invasion of Greece, two Italian soldiers guarded a bridge near their tent.

Italian soldiers took up defensive positions in the snow while stationed in Greece during the winter of 1940–1941.

Italian engineers tried to repair a road and small bridge blown up by Greek troops.

Common World War II Weapons

World War II saw the development of more efficient, more deadly arms. Major advances in production and technology created small arms that had their own legacy.

1. The **Walther P38** was Germany's successor to the Luger. It quickly became popular with German forces, as well as with Allied troops who tried to capture the Walther and use it in place of their own sidearm.

2. Model 24 Stielhandgranate, the German stick grenade, was sometimes called a "potato masher" by the British. Used in both world wars, the Stielhandgranate had a TNT charge mounted on the handle and could be thrown further than a round hand grenade.

3. The **Thompson M1928A1** earned a reputation as a gangster's firearm because it had been used by crooks in the United States. Later, it became an iconic gun of American GIs. The Thompson had a high rate of fire, with powerful .45 caliber rounds.

4. The **Browning Automatic Rifle (BAR)** provided American infantry squads with a weapon that was lighter than a machine gun and had a higher rate of fire than other rifles (550 rounds per minute). The Browning saw action in the islands of the Pacific, North Africa, and in Europe.

5. The **Mk 2 fragmentation grenade**, known as the "pineapple grenade," was standard issue to American soldiers during the war.

◄ 1. Walther P38

▲ 2. Standard German hand grenade

▼ 4. Browning automatic rifle

◄ 6. Colt M1911A1

▼ 9. Japanese Arisaka Type 99 Rifle and Bayonet

▲ 11. German MG 42 machine gun

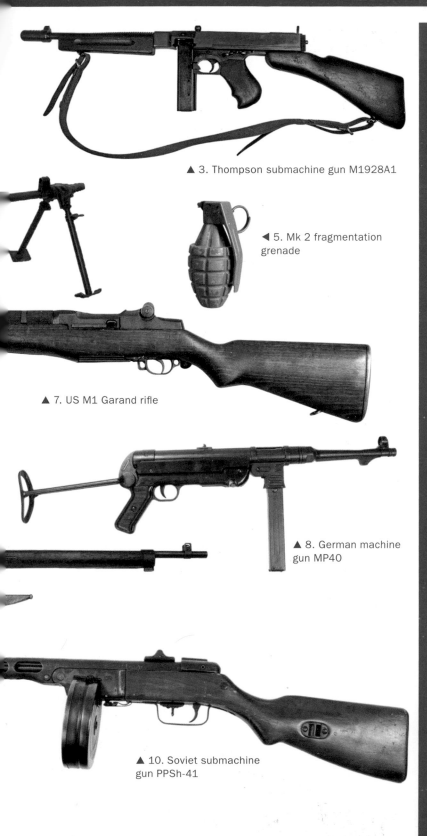

▲ 3. Thompson submachine gun M1928A1

◄ 5. Mk 2 fragmentation grenade

▲ 7. US M1 Garand rifle

▲ 8. German machine gun MP40

▲ 10. Soviet submachine gun PPSh-41

6. Possibly the most successful handgun ever, the **American Colt M1911A1**, a .45 caliber pistol, was the standard issue U.S. sidearm from 1911 until 1990. It is still in use today with special forces units.

7. Providing accuracy, power, and a high rate of fire, the **M1 Garand** was the standard rifle of American troops from 1936 to the 1960s. General George Patton called it the greatest battle implement ever devised, a belief that has been echoed by both veterans and historians. The rifle gave troops the ability to fire eight .30 caliber rounds as quickly as they could pull the trigger.

8. Considered to be the trademark German weapon throughout the war, the **MP40** had all-metal construction and stampable parts. It replaced the earlier MP38 and became the primary submachine gun of the Wehrmacht.

9. The **Japanese Arisaka Type 99 rifle** was used by the Imperial Japanese Army from 1907 to the end of the war. The rifle fired a low-powered 6.5 mm bullet but was somewhat longer than most rifles. The longer reach gave an advantage to Japanese soldiers, who were usually smaller in stature than their Western enemies.

10. The **Soviet PPSh-41** was a retooling of an earlier submachine gun that had stamped parts, making mass production easy. The PPSh had a 71-round drum magazine and could fire 900 rounds a minute, making it a deadly adversary.

11. The **MG 42**, which was produced by Mauser, combined German engineering with the drive to create a perfect machine gun. Known for its distinct tearing sound, the MG 42 was first used in 1942 in both Africa and in Russia. The machine gun could fire 1,200 rounds per minute, the highest rate of fire of any infantry machine gun. The MG 42 still serves as a model for current-day machine guns.

4 | WAR TO THE EAST AND WEST

1941: GERMANY HAD ANNEXED ITS SMALLER NEIGHBORS AND WAS READY TO MOVE EAST. IN THE PACIFIC, THE JAPANESE WAR MACHINE WAS ON THE MOVE AS WELL.

On December 7, 1941, the Japanese bombed Wheeler Field on Honolulu. Dozens of aircraft were destroyed during the initial bombing raids.

"Yesterday, December 7, 1941—a date which will live in infamy . . ."

—Franklin D. Roosevelt, December 8, 1941

By early February 1941, British and Australian forces had captured half of Libya and taken more than 130,000 prisoners.

V for Victory

Soon after the war began, Victor de Laveleye, director of the French-speaking Belgian broadcasts for the BBC, decided that the Allies needed a sign to inspire soldiers and the public. He suggested that holding up the first two fingers would symbolize "V for Victory." Winston Churchill (above) waved to a crowd using the new sign, which soon became a rallying gesture throughout the world.

1941

Italian and German Forces in North Africa

THE DESERT FOX DEFIED ORDERS, ROUTED THE ALLIES, AND CAPTURED TOBRUK, LIBYA.

By the end of 1940, the British-led tank corps had expelled the Italians from Egypt, and some Allied armored forces were diverted to fight Italian forces in the East African territory that included British Somaliland. The remaining Seventh Armored Division continued west into Libya.

Italian leader Benito Mussolini requested help, and Reich Chancellor Adolf Hitler chose Commander Erwin Rommel to lead an expeditionary force, the Afrika Korps, to support the Italians. Rommel was told to hold the Allies at bay, but once in Libya, he began pushing the Allies back to the Egyptian border. The Axis powers were soon winning.

German tanks moved through Cyrenaica, Libya, in April 1941.

Axis Troops on the Move

In 1941, Axis forces moved east into Russia, south into Greece, and into North Africa.

JAN

JANUARY 22 The Allies took Tobruk, Libya.

MARCH 11 Roosevelt signed the Lend-Lease Act to provide Allies with matériel.

MARCH

MARCH 24 Rommel began an attack near El Agheila, Libya.

MAY

MAY 24 The *Bismarck* destroyed the HMS *Hood*, the pride of the Royal Navy.

JUNE

JUNE 22 Four million Axis soldiers entered the USSR, the largest invasion in the history of warfare.

DECEMBER 7 Japanese forces attacked Pearl Harbor.

DECEMBER 8 The U.S. declared war on Japan.

DECEMBER 11 Germany and Italy declared war on the U.S.

DEC

DECEMBER 23 U.S. territory Wake Island fell to the Japanese.

Erwin Rommel, the Desert Fox

Erwin Rommel (1891–1944), who was appointed field marshall in mid-1942, earned the name "Desert Fox" because of his ability to outsmart the enemy on the battlefield, especially during the North African campaign.

Rommel arrived in Libya in February 1941, with instructions to hold the line and not to wage major offensive efforts. Rommel had other ideas; despite orders from both Germany and Italy, he advanced his forces and captured the region surrounding Tobruk in June 1941. Rommel's Afrika Korps was known for stealth and surprise. He was famous for moving whole divisions during storms or at night to gain advantage on the battlefield.

Rommel, by all accounts, was a man of stellar character, who treated his troops and prisoners of war humanely. He refused to murder Jews. Rommel was implicated in the plot to assassinate Hitler in 1944. Hitler allowed Rommel to commit suicide, and Rommel ended his life on October 14, 1944.

1941

Operation Crusader: Holding On to a Crucial Port Town

AN EPIC TANK CONFRONTATION IN LIBYA WOULD BE DECIDED NOT BY TACTICS AND POWER, BUT BY LOGISTICS.

In late November, the Allies launched a major offensive to assist the Australians who had been under siege in Tobruk for eight months. Holding the town and its port was vital to the Allies' strategy because it forced the Axis powers to bring supplies overland, across 930 miles of desert, and would hamper their ability to advance to the Suez Canal. The Allies were able to move close to, but not reach, the besieged city because Axis presence in the region was too strong. Nevertheless, Rommel's attempt to secure an alternate port on the Egyptian coast failed. Informed by the Italians that the supply problems would continue for some time, Rommel withdrew from the Mediterranean shore to a more easily-defensible inland position. The move handed victory to the Allies in Tobruk and brought the siege there to an end. Battles between the Axis and Allied forces in North Africa would continue for the next two years, with victories seesawing back and forth between the two sides.

Under Field Marshal Erwin Rommel's command, German troops proved to be strong adversaries as they fought against the Allies during the siege of Tobruk.

Allied forces used sand tables to predict German troop movement and to plan their own countermoves in Tobruk in November 1941.

Allied soldiers took cover behind a low wall as they fought back against the Axis forces during the siege of Tobruk.

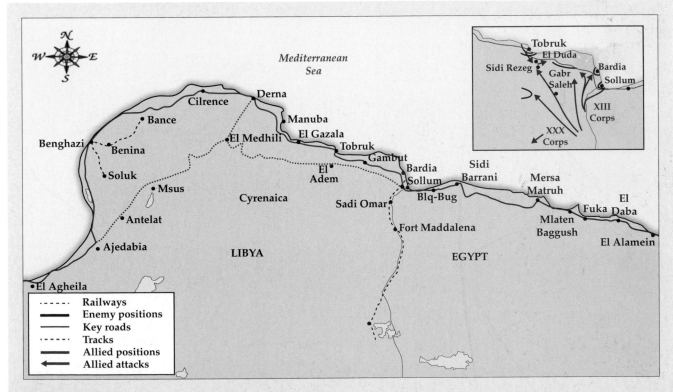

Battle for Tobruk

Tobruk occupied a key location on the Mediterranean Sea, and both Allied and Axis powers were determined to control it.

After Yugoslavia signed the Tripartite Pact with Nazi Germany on March 25, 1941, military officers organized a coup d'état. Two days later, King Peter II (right) was installed on the throne. One month later, Peter was deposed.

A German soldier stood guard while Serbian prisoners were rounded up following their surrender.

Through Yugoslavia to Greece

German forces moved quickly through Bulgaria to Yugoslavia and then into Greece.

On April 24, 1941, German soldiers arrived in Zagreb, under the pretext of protecting the Croatians from the Serbs.

Between September and November 1941, over 5,000 Yugoslavians were executed.

1941

Germany Seizes Yugoslavia

A NAZI NEIGHBOR HAD THE MISFORTUNE OF STANDING BETWEEN HITLER AND HIS NEW TARGET, THE NATION OF GREECE.

On April 6, 1941, Hitler ordered German forces, along with their Italian, Romanian, Hungarian, and Bulgarian Axis allies, to invade Yugoslavia and Greece. In a blitzkrieg of armored and motorized attacks, the Germans pummeled Yugoslavia's capital, Belgrade, and struck the nation from three sides. Yugoslavia,

debilitated by political instability and ethnic divisions, was no match for the efficient Axis military. The country's air force was almost completely destroyed during the first hours of fighting, and the leaders were forced into surrender on April 17, less than two weeks after the initial assault.

Hitler may not have wanted to actually occupy Yugoslavia or to take the territory, but he did want to use it as a staging ground for attacking his next target, Greece. There was also a bonus: By winning control of Yugoslavia, which was then divided and occupied, the Nazis secured an important source of raw materials for Germany's war effort.

German forces built temporary bridges and also used small boats to cross the Pinios River near Larissa in northern Greece.

Faces of War

In a speech made at the Reichstag in 1941, Hitler expressed his admiration for the Greek resistance, saying of the campaign, "Historical justice, however, obliges me to state . . . the Greek soldier fought with the highest courage. He capitulated only when further resistance had become impossible . . ."

1941

Operation Marita: Germany Invades Greece

THE GREEKS HAD REPELLED ATTACKS BY ITALY, BUT THEY HAD NO REALISTIC HOPE OF RESISTING THE WEHRMACHT.

Greece had successfully defended itself against the Italian invasion in October 1940 and again in March 1941. But when the Germans launched Operation Marita, an attack through Bulgaria starting April 6, 1941, the majority of Greek forces were still fighting the Italians in Albania. Facing a second war front, the Greek army was vastly outnumbered, even with some 60,000 British reinforcements sent to help out. An intensive Luftwaffe bombing campaign, followed by the rapid advance of tank forces, pushed the Greek troops back quickly.

By April 21, the Greek soldiers in Albania were cut off from the rest of their country and forced to surrender. Six days later, the Germans entered Athens, and Greece fell to the Axis countries.

In April 1941, German forces used prison labor to build dykes and bridges to allow their tanks and troops to cross rivers.

German paratroopers met stiff resistance from Allied forces during the invasion of Crete. Because rifles were dropped in separate containers, paratroopers were armed only with knives and pistols when they hit the ground.

Operation Mercury: Crete

Fleeing the German advance in Greece, the remaining Greek and British Empire troops evacuated 60 miles south to the island of Crete. The location contained valuable airfields and was coveted by both sides. Since the British Royal Navy was the dominant power in the Mediterranean, the Germans decided an amphibious assault was not worth the risk.

Instead, beginning on May 20, 1941, the Germans attempted to take Crete with huge numbers of paratroopers and troops flown in on gliders. In executing Operation Mercury, the attackers were slow-moving and suffered heavy losses, but they eventually gained a foothold on the tiny island. Within seven days, the Allied commanders evacuated. Greek King George II and his cabinet fled to Cairo, and by June 1, Crete was occupied by the Germans. Now, all of the Balkans were firmly under German control. The Greek government would remain in Cairo until October 1944, when the occupiers finally withdrew.

Operation Mercury was a complete victory for Germany, but it has also been described as disastrous. The country's troops suffered heavily, with approximately 4,000 men dying in the battle, and another 2,600 sustaining wounds.

Allies Get Out

Between April 24 and April 30, 1941, over 50,000 Allied soldiers were evacuated from Greece. The soldiers came from a number of different countries, including Australia, New Zealand, Britain, and Poland. As part of the evacuation, the Allies were forced to leave behind aircraft, trucks, and weapons.

Reich Chancellor Adolf Hitler visited the *Bismarck* on May 5, 1941, just before the ship took to sea to fight in the Battle of the Atlantic.

1941

The Battle of the Atlantic

CONTROL OF THE SEAS AND OF THE SHIPPING LANES WAS VITAL TO BOTH THE ALLIES AND THE AXIS POWERS.

The Battle of the Atlantic, for the crucial shipping lanes between North America and Britain, began in the mid-1940s and did not end until 1943. Because the routes were used to deliver food, raw materials, equipment, munitions, and oil to the English, the three-year fight to secure their control was critical for Allied success. The German military attempted to demolish the naval highway with both surface ships and submarines, known as "U-boats," as well as with mines and aircraft. Over time, the Germans managed to sink several million tons of freight, even as the Allies responded with naval convoys of merchant and civilian ships. In May 1941, a German U-boat sank the USS *Robin Moore*, a merchant ship, and even though all aboard survived, the incident angered President Franklin Roosevelt, who called it an act of intimidation. Then on October 31, 1941, an American destroyer, the USS *Reuben James*, was torpedoed and sank, killing 115 crew members. These two incidents served to further draw the United States into the Battle of the Atlantic.

Officers on the bridge of a British naval destroyer watched for enemy ships that might be prowling the Atlantic in October 1941.

Prime Minister Winston Churchill thanked merchant ship crews and dockworkers in Liverpool for their role in the Battle of the Atlantic.

The Enigma Machine

German military signals were passed using special encryption devices called "Enigma machines." In the 1920s, a German military engineer named Arthur Scherbius had developed the device, which used electro-mechanical rotors for coding and decoding messages. Because of the rotors, cracking codes generated by Enigma machines was almost impossible, and even the best British and American cryptologists and mathematicians were unable to accomplish the complicated task.

On May 9, 1941, the Royal Navy captured U-boat U-110 and secured its Enigma machine, codes, and codebooks. The Germans were led to believe that the U-boat had sunk.

Cryptologists worked nonstop at Bletchley Park, an estate in Milton Keynes, England, to decipher the material. They also worked carefully so that the Germans would not realize that the Enigma codes had been cracked.

It took nearly three years to construct the *Bismarck*, and it was the heaviest ship built by any of the European nations. Its crew numbered more than 2,200.

1941

The Sinking of the *Bismarck*

HITLER BELIEVED THAT WITH POWERFUL NEW SHIPS, GERMANY WOULD WIN THE WAR AT SEA. IT WAS A SHORT-LIVED DREAM.

The Allies feared the German battleship *Bismarck*—and with good reason. The warship, one of the largest built by a European power, had armor-plated sides, accurate heavy guns, and had recorded speeds of 30 knots in sea trials.

Eight minutes into the *Bismarck*'s first engagement, on May 24, it sank the HMS *Hood*, the pride of the Royal Navy. The *Bismarck* also forced another Allied battleship, the HMS *Prince of Wales*, to retreat. Damaged in the battles, the *Bismarck* changed course and moved toward occupied France for repairs.

> **"The loss of H.M.S. *Hood* and her company has thus been avenged . . ."**
> —British Board of Admiralty, 1941

The British committed every possible resource to finding the behemoth, and within two days, it was spotted by a British aircraft. That evening, a British plane struck the ship's rudder with a torpedo. Unable to steer, the *Bismarck* became an easy target for the British fleet, which fired repeatedly into the crippled ship. Finally, after taking more than 400 shells and three torpedoes, the *Bismarck* sank on May 27. British cruisers involved in the attack were unharmed, and two British destroyers sustained only minor damage.

After being attacked by the *Bismarck*, the British battle cruiser *Hood* sank very quickly. The battle on May 24 lasted less than 30 minutes.

After the *Bismarck* was destroyed on May 27, British ships picked up about 110 of its crew members, some of whom are shown here.

1. USS *ARIZONA*

4. HMS *ARK ROYAL*

7. HMS *VICTORIOUS*

World War II Warships

Before the outbreak of World War II, Britain and Japan had the most powerful navies in the world. As other major powers geared up for global conflict, they began expanding their fleets as well, adding battleships, light and heavy cruisers, aircraft carriers, and destroyers. All would play a major role in the war.

2. USS *IOWA*

3. *KAGA*, IMPERIAL JAPANESE NAVY

5. *YAMATO*, IMPERIAL JAPANESE NAVY

6. AMERICAN DESTROYER ESCORT

8. GERMAN U-BOAT

1. The battleship USS *Arizona* in 1918 led the U.S. fleet in a naval review as it returned from World War I. In December 1941, it was sunk at Pearl Harbor. 2. The battleship USS *Iowa* spent her first years in the Atlantic. 3. Japan's aircraft carrier, the *Kaga*, took part in the attack on Pearl Harbor and was destroyed during the Battle of Midway. 4. The British Royal Navy aircraft carrier HMS *Ark Royal* carried the scout planes that spotted the *Bismarck*. 5. The Japanese warship *Yamato* was ranked among the fiercest of the era; it was sunk by U.S. aircraft in 1945. 6. Destroyer escorts were smaller than the normal American destroyers and were designed for convoy protection. 7. The HMS *Victorious*, an aircraft carrier, helped hunt the *Bismarck*, and it then supported Arctic convoys. For several years during the war, the British ship was on loan to the U.S. 8. German U-boat 16 took part in the first Battle of the Atlantic and after being attacked by British ships, sank in October 1939.

1941

Operation Barbarossa: Germany Assaults the USSR

STALIN STOOD BY PASSIVELY AS HITLER
MOUNTED THE LARGEST INVASION IN HISTORY.

When Hitler and Soviet Premier Joseph Stalin signed the Nazi-Soviet Nonaggression Pact in 1939, Germany had hoped to avoid a two-front war by ceding land in Poland and the Balkans to the Soviets. However, the pact was broken less than two years later with an assault known as Operation Barbarossa. Starting June 22, 1941, Hitler unleashed the full might of the German military in a blitzkrieg—a style of war Germany had been perfecting in the Balkans—against Russia.

Having spent a decade re-arming Germany's military forces, Hitler was able to send three entire armies, almost four million troops, east in the attack. It was the largest invasion in the history of warfare, and German soldiers spread along an 1,800-mile-long front. They brought with them close to 3,500 tanks, over 500,000 motor vehicles, and 750,000 horses.

Yet, in spite of the Germans' expertise, their logistical preparations would prove to be insufficient. In addition, Germany's industrial base was not yet ready to support a long war and was unable to provide needed supplies. Operation Barbarossa would play a pivotal role in deciding the outcome of the war, and during the ensuing months, Russia would lose millions of people, both civilians and military.

By the end of October 1941, the German invasion was well underway. Here, German tanks advanced on an undefended Soviet village.

Using flamethrowers, German soldiers attacked a bunker during Operation Barbarossa.

German tanks and crew met little opposition as they crossed rivers and advanced into Russia.

In battle, German troops used flamethrowers, developed by German engineers in the early 1900s, as well as flametanks.

The March to Leningrad

The German invasion of Russia had begun with massive air strikes. On land, the Germans mobilized three formations. Army Group North moved into Lithuania, driving toward Leningrad. Army Group Centre marched through Poland and then turned toward Moscow. Meanwhile, Army Group South attacked the Ukraine and its economic centers.

Stalin ordered his troops not to surrender or retreat, which prevented the Russians from falling back and forming stronger unified defenses. The Germans easily breached the thin Soviet lines and captured entire Russian armies, taking more than three million prisoners in 1941 alone. Many of these prisoners later died of starvation, part of Hitler's plan to clear eastern Europe for German colonization.

A German soldier, armed with a gun and hand grenade, defended his position during the winter of 1941.

Russian soldiers, dressed in winter camouflage, fought hard but with little success during the winter of 1941.

1941

Operation Typhoon: The Battle of Moscow

THE GERMANS HAD TO MOVE QUICKLY
TO CAPTURE MOSCOW BEFORE WINTER SET IN.

Moscow was the primary target of Operation Barbarossa, but German progress, impeded by poor roads and bad weather, slowed as troops moved toward the Russian capital. By late October, the Germans were 40 miles from Moscow and both sides had suffered huge losses. Civilians living in Moscow committed themselves to the war effort and helped the Soviet army build defenses for the city. In addition, 25 Soviet divisions were transferred to the capital from Siberia.

When winter arrived in November, German forces were still in summer uniforms. They had expected a fast victory but could no longer hold out in the cold. As the Germans debated a withdrawal, the Russians launched a counterattack and drove the Germans back. A further assault on Moscow during the winter was out of the question.

Before heading into battle to defend Moscow on November 7, 1941, Soviet soldiers first staged a traditional military parade in Red Square.

In an attempt to defend the capital, Russian soldiers mounted antiaircraft guns in the streets of Moscow.

A light-armored division made its way from Moscow to the front, a journey of about 40 miles.

Fighting from street to street, Red Army troops battled over the town of Yukhnov, about 130 miles southwest of Moscow.

Troops used and faced heavy gunfire during the fighting at Murmansk.

1941

Operation Silver Fox: Germany and Finland Invade Russia

THE NAZIS NEEDED ANOTHER PORT CITY,
AND THEY HOPED THAT SOVIET FORCES
COULD NOT MOBILIZE ALONG TWO FRONTS.

A week after Operation Barbarossa was launched on the Eastern Front, a second assault on Russia began, this time in the north. On June 29, Germans and Finns entered Russia from Finland. Their goal was to capture the key port of Murmansk and its railway, which was critical to supplying Russian troops. The invading soldiers, expecting that Russia would have diverted its forces away from Murmansk to support the main military operation in the south, anticipated light resistance.

Yet the Russians fought hard, made excellent use of the terrain, and defended themselves against the assault. Caught off guard by the determined opposition and the oncoming winter, the Finns and Germans called off the assault in November. Shortly thereafter, supplies to Russia began arriving again in Murmansk, which helped the Soviets recover from losses sustained during the year.

The Royal Air Force helped in the battle at
Murmansk, defending the airfield at nearby Vaenga.

Soviet soldiers often faced wet, muddy
conditions during the fighting at Murmansk.

1941

Rapidly Closing in on Pearl Harbor

BY NOVEMBER 26, 1941, A JAPANESE FLEET INCLUDING SIX AIRCRAFT
CARRIERS AND 11 DESTROYERS SAT 275 MILES NORTH OF HAWAII.

To sustain its war effort, Japan needed oil and other natural resources and began looking to secure them from the resource-rich territories of Southeast Asia. There was a complicating factor, however: Though it was paramount to Japan's political and military leaders for troops to move unopposed through Southeast Asia, it was becoming clear that conflict between Japan and the United States was inevitable.

Japan's Admiral Isoroku Yamamoto decided that the best way to avoid—or

> **"We should do our best to decide the fate of the war on the very first day."**
>
> —Isoroku Yamamoto

to win—a war with the U.S. was to immobilize the U.S. Pacific Fleet, and to do that, he intended to annihilate the armada in a surprise attack. He convinced Emperor Hirohito that a preemptive assault on the Pacific Fleet based at the Pearl Harbor Naval Base would cripple the flotilla and prevent the U.S. from countering Japan's territorial expansion. In October 1941, the plan was approved, and soon thereafter, after intense and careful planning, the Japanese fleet began moving toward Hawaii.

On the morning of December 7, Japanese pilots received their final instructions before beginning their bombing runs over Pearl Harbor.

The Japanese Zero, or *Reisen Kanjikisen,* could carry two 132-pound bombs under its wings; for a time, it could outmaneuver any other airplanes it fought.

Pearl Harbor, just before the attack

Why Did Japan Attack Pearl Harbor?

While the attack on the U.S. Naval Base in Pearl Harbor took most Americans by surprise, tensions between Japan and the U.S. over oil had been rising for some time.

In 1940, attempting to curb further Japanese military expansion into Manchuria and Indochina, the U.S. prohibited exports of steel, scrap iron, and aviation fuel to Japan. In July 1941, the U.S. broadened the effort by ceasing all oil exports. Given oil's importance to the Japanese economy, many of that country's officials viewed the U.S. ban as an undeclared act of war.

Oil was available in Malaysia, but to reach it, the Japanese would have to overcome U.S. naval forces in Pearl Harbor. Prime Minister Tojo directed Admiral Yamamoto to plan an attack to cripple the U.S. fleet.

Japan's Dependence on Imported Oil

In 1940, the country imported more than 90 percent of its oil from two countries.

United States
Between 3,820,000 and 4,366,000 metric tons, or 80 percent

Dutch East India (Indonesia)
Between 621,000 and 709,000 metric tons, or 13 percent

This photograph of smoke rising over Pearl Harbor was recovered from a Japanese plane later captured by U.S. forces.

Honolulu Star-Bulletin 1ˢᵗ EXTRA

WAR!
OAHU BOMBED BY JAPANESE PLANES

SAN FRANCISCO, Dec. 7.— President Roosevelt announced this morning that Japanese planes had attacked Manila and Pearl Harbor.

Who Knew What When

Soon after the devastating attack on Pearl Harbor, conspiracy theorists argued that the U.S. government not only knew about the Japanese plan ahead of time, they allowed it to happen to create a pretext for the United States to enter World War II.

Ten official inquiries conducted years after the end of the war concluded that mistakes and bureaucratic bungling resulted in the U.S. intelligence failure to predict the devastating attack.

1941

Pearl Harbor: The Attack Begins

AT 7:55 A.M. ON SUNDAY, DECEMBER 7, 1941, THE FIRST WAVE OF JAPANESE DIVE-BOMBERS BEGAN THEIR DEVASTATING RAID.

In just under two hours of Japanese bombardment at Pearl Harbor, eight U.S. battleships were either very badly damaged or sank, and three cruisers and three destroyers had been damaged. In addition, more than 180 aircraft had been destroyed. More than 2,300 military personnel were killed, and over 1,000 more had been wounded.

The Japanese sustained some losses as well, but they were relatively minor— between 29 and 60 of the 360 airplanes flown in battle that day, a couple of submarines, and fewer than 100 men. The attack horrified Americans, and on December 8, the U.S. Congress declared war on Japan.

Japanese planes attacked Ford Naval Air Station, where 33 planes were destroyed or damaged. The U.S. lost nearly 300 planes, either destroyed or damaged, during the raid.

During the second wave of bombings, Japanese planes met a wall of antiaircraft fire.

The USS *California* was torpedoed in the early minutes of the attack. The ship sank and nearly 100 of the crew were killed in the battle.

Both the USS *Cassin* and *Downes* were in dry dock on December 7. The *Cassin* capsized, and both ships were nearly destroyed.

At 8:06 a.m., the USS *Arizona* was hit. Moments later, the ship's powder magazines and fuel stores exploded, causing huge fires. Only 334 of the crew survived; 1,177 sailors and marines were killed.

President Franklin D. Roosevelt addressed Congress on December 8, 1941.

1941

"A Date Which Will Live In Infamy"

IN THE WAKE OF THE PEARL HARBOR ATTACKS, FRANKLIN D. ROOSEVELT GAVE ONE OF THE MOST MEMORABLE SPEECHES IN U.S. HISTORY.

"Yesterday, December 7, 1941—a date which will live in infamy—the United States of America was suddenly and deliberately attacked by naval and air forces of the Empire of Japan.

The United States was at peace with that nation, and, at the solicitation of Japan, was still in conversation with its government and its emperor looking toward the maintenance of peace in the Pacific. Indeed, one hour after Japanese air squadrons had commenced bombing in the American island of Oahu, the Japanese ambassador to the United States and his colleague delivered to our Secretary of State a formal reply to a recent American message. While this reply stated that it seemed useless to continue the existing diplomatic negotiations, it contained no threat or hint of war or of armed attack.

It will be recorded that the distance of Hawaii from Japan makes it obvious that the attack was deliberately planned many days or even weeks ago. During the intervening time the Japanese government has deliberately sought to deceive the United States by false statements and expressions of hope for continued peace."

—Franklin D. Roosevelt, December 8, 1941

From Civilian Life to the Military

Newspapers across the nation rushed out extra editions to announce the United States' entry into the war. After Pearl Harbor, thousands of men and women left their homes and civilian life to join the war effort. By late 1942, all men aged 18 to 64 were required to register for the draft. New recruits came from every state and from every economic and social strata. The majority were assigned to the U.S. Army.

1941

The Main Players at Pearl Harbor

THE CAREERS OF THE POLITICAL AND MILITARY FIGURES WHO PLANNED
AND RESPONDED TO THE ATTACK FOLLOWED UNPREDICTABLE PATHS.

Husband E. Kimmel

Admiral Husband E. Kimmel (1882–1968) graduated from the U.S. Naval Academy in 1904, and in 1915, he was named aide to the Assistant Secretary of the Navy, Franklin D. Roosevelt. Kimmel served on several U.S. battleships during World War I. When World War II began, he held the rank of rear admiral and was commander of the cruiser force at Pearl Harbor. In early 1941, Kimmel was appointed commander of the Pacific Fleet. The admiral had been advised in October that war might begin with a surprise attack on Pearl Harbor, but it is said that Kimmel did not think that the Japanese would strike Hawaii. Following the attack on Pearl Harbor, Kimmel was relieved of fleet command and reduced in rank. He retired from the military in early 1942. In 1999, the U.S. Senate passed a resolution saying that Kimmel had performed his duties competently and professionally.

Walter C. Short

Lt. General Walter Short (1880–1949) was appointed head of the U.S. Army's Hawaiian Department in February 1941 and was responsible for defending U.S. military installations in Hawaii at the time of the Pearl Harbor bombing. Prior to his appointment in Hawaii, Short had served as an assistant chief of staff for training of the Third Army. According to some, Short saw his mission goal to be that of training, and it was his defense tactic of lining up warplanes wingtip to wingtip that proved disastrous. Short may not have believed that the Japanese would attack Pearl Harbor, and some say that he failed to heed war warnings that were issued on November 27, 1941. Short was reduced in rank shortly after the attack and retired from the military in early 1942. During several years of investigations, Short maintained that he was not guilty of dereliction of duty. In 1999, the U.S. Senate passed a resolution saying that Short had performed his duties competently and professionally.

Hideki Tojo

General Hideki Tojo (1884–1948) was an accomplished military officer and statesman. At the end of World War I, he served for a short time as a military attaché in Berlin. He then served as chief of staff for the army during the Japanese invasion of Manchuria. He was named vice minister of war in 1938 and became prime minister in 1941. An aggressive militarist, Tojo was responsible for the attack on Pearl Harbor, and afterward, he led Japan's war efforts.

USS *Arizona* Memorial

The USS *Arizona* Memorial in Pearl Harbor was erected over the sunken battleship and is the final resting place of the ship's 1,177 crew members who lost their lives during the attack. The memorial had humble beginnings. In 1950, Admiral Arthur Radford ordered a flagpole to be erected over the sunken battleship. Several years later, a plaque was mounted at the flagpole's base. Then, in 1958, President Dwight Eisenhower approved creation of the memorial; completed in 1961, it was dedicated in 1962.

The memorial has come to honor all the military personnel killed at Pearl Harbor, some 2,400, most of whom died within the first 90 minutes of the assault.

Henry L. Stimson

Henry Stimson (1867–1950) served as secretary of war from July 10, 1940, until September 21, 1945. During those years, he was responsible for the recruitment and training of 13 million servicemen, and he helped formulate the nation's war strategy. In his diary a few days before the attack on Pearl Harbor, Stimson recorded his concerns about how the United States would respond to a surprise attack by the Japanese.

Franklin Delano Roosevelt

U.S. President Franklin D. Roosevelt (1882–1945) faced strong internal opposition to involving the U.S. in the war, but he was committed to helping Britain, France, and China stand up against their aggressors. The "Arsenal of Democracy" rearmament program provided Roosevelt the means to prepare the U.S. military for war.

The assault at Pearl Harbor gave him the ammunition he needed to persuade the nation to officially join the war effort. Roosevelt died less than one month before V-E Day.

Captain Mitsuo Fuchida

Captain Mitsuo Fuchida (1902–1976) was the airstrike leader of the Japanese carrier force that targeted Pearl Harbor. At the time, he held the rank of commander. Fuchida had a reputation as a skilled pilot and had participated in air attacks over China in the 1930s. On December 7, he took off from the *Akagi* and led the first wave of planes over Pearl Harbor. It is said that just before the first bombs were dropped, he transmitted a message to his commanders that the attack was a surprise. Fuchida was also on the *Akagi* during the attack at Midway, where he was injured.

Vice Admiral Chuichi Nagumo

Chuichi Nagumo (1887–1944) was a torpedo specialist in the Imperial Japanese Navy. He commanded the Japanese carrier strike force that attacked Pearl Harbor and carried out raids in the South Pacific during early 1942. Following the bombing of Pearl Harbor, Nagumo was criticized by some for not following up with a final attack on the oil tanks and naval facilities in Oahu. In June 1942, Nagumo lost four aircraft carriers at Midway, but he retained command of the remaining carriers fighting in the battles in the eastern Solomons and in the Santa Cruz Islands until November 1942. He then retained control of a smaller Japanese fleet in the Marianas Island region. Nagumo was still active in the war in the Pacific in July 1944 when he took his own life during the Battle of Saipan.

Isoroku Yamamoto

Isoroku Yamamoto (1884–1943) was a marshal admiral and commander in chief of the Japanese Combined Fleet during the attack on Pearl Harbor. Yamamoto pushed for the development of naval aviation, the centerpiece of Japan's ability to strike long-distance targets. Yamamoto personally helped to plan the attack on Pearl Harbor. He died on an inspection flight over the South Pacific when American fighters shot down his plane.

Approximately 80,000 Allied forces were taken prisoner when Singapore was seized by the Japanese in February 1942. The fighting lasted just one week, from February 8 to the 15th.

1941

The Japanese Set Their Sights on Southeast Asia

THAILAND, HONG KONG, THE PHILIPPINES, AND OTHERS WERE TARGETED FOR THEIR OIL SUPPLIES.

While the attack on Pearl Harbor was taking place, the Japanese launched invasions of Thailand, Hong Kong, the Philippines, the British-controlled states of Malaya, and the Dutch East Indies. Their prime target was the Dutch East Indies, a major source of oil in the region.

The other nations were chosen for different strategic reasons. Malaya would be a significant source of raw materials. Hong Kong had a needed port, and Thai railways and coastline were vital for transporting goods. The Philippines had air bases and immense strategic value. The Japanese invaded the archipelago the day after Pearl Harbor and occupied it for the next three years.

Japanese forces mounted a vigorous campaign against Allied forces in Hong Kong. The British surrendered the colony on Christmas Day, less than three weeks after the battle began.

Japanese soldiers cheered after defeating British troops in Hong Kong.

5 | ATTACK AND COUNTERATTACK

1942: A HARSH WINTER AND DETERMINED OPPOSITION SLOWED THE AXIS CONQUEST OF EUROPE, WHILE EVENTS AT MIDWAY GAVE THE ALLIES AN ADVANTAGE IN THE PACIFIC.

Men from the British Royal Air Force worked together stacking mines at a munitions store in England. The weapons would soon be put to use.

"They sowed the wind, and now they are going to reap the whirlwind."

—British Air Marshal Arthur "Bomber" Harris, paraphrasing the Bible about the British response to the Nazis

1942

Hitler Pushes on in Russia

GERMANY COVETED THE CAUCASUS ON THE EASTERN FRONT AND FORGED AHEAD TO CONQUER THE AREA.

Benito Mussolini and Chancellor Adolf Hitler met on the Russian front in 1942 to discuss their war plans.

One of Chancellor Adolf Hitler's primary objectives when World War II began in 1939 was to avoid a war on two fronts, and until his troops invaded the Soviet Union in June 1941, he had largely achieved that goal. The Red Army, however, was unexpectedly tenacious, and fighting in the eastern regions of the country, especially near Leningrad, dragged on through late 1941 and throughout 1942. At the same time, despite the Blitz and the ongoing Battle of the Atlantic, Britain was continuing to fight, leaving Germany exactly where Hitler did not want it to be: facing foes on the Eastern and Western Fronts. The Nazis were undeterred, and by 1942, they had captured vast regions of the Soviet Union and were resolved to conquer the Soviets at any cost.

Fierce Fighting, Slow Progress

Fierce battles took place across the European and Pacific theaters in 1942. But the course of the war was starting to change.

JANUARY 20 The Wannsee Conference was held in a Berlin suburb to plan the extermination of the Jews.

▲ **JANUARY 26** The first American troops landed in Europe, arriving in Northern Ireland.

FEBRUARY 19 Roosevelt signed Executive Order 9066, allowing the War Department to exclude anyone perceived to be a threat from designated military areas. Japanese Americans were targeted on the West Coast, while German and Italian Americans were targeted on the East Coast.

MARCH 26 Jews living in Berlin were forced to clearly identify their homes.

1942   **JANUARY** • • • • **FEBRUARY** • • • • **MARCH** • • • •

Russian trucks had to cross destroyed roads as they made their way through the Caucasus.

German troops used horse-drawn wagons to transport supplies. Others repaired roads on the muddy ground of the Soviet Union.

▲ **APRIL 9** The Bataan Peninsula, in the Philippines, fell to the Japanese, and the "Bataan Death March" began on April 10.

APRIL 18 Lt. Col. James Doolittle led a raid on Japan, bombing Tokyo and other cities.

MAY 7–8 The first air-naval battle in history took place as Japan and the United States faced each other in the Coral Sea.

JUNE 4–7 The Battle of Midway raged between the U.S. and Japan. The U.S. victory marked a turning point in the war.

NOVEMBER 19 Soviet forces launched Operation Uranus to counterattack German forces at Stalingrad.

• **APRIL** • • • • • **MAY** • • • • • **JUNE** • • • • • • **NOVEMBER**

Sevastopol, a heavily fortified Russian naval base, quickly fell to the Germans, who entered the port city on June 30, 1942.

Germany Begins to Falter

By early 1942, cracks in the German offense had begun to appear. Operation Barbarossa had started strongly, and after a number of early victories, it appeared that the Nazis were poised to capture Moscow and Leningrad. Instead, Operation Barbarossa stalled on the outskirts of Moscow. The Nazis discovered as they moved forward that the Russians had destroyed everything in the German path, including harvested crops and livestock. Buildings had been blown up, leaving nothing for the advancing, poorly supplied Germans.

Victory and Costly Errors

Hitler was largely to blame for what unfolded in Moscow. Spurning the advice of his generals, Hitler decided to divert forces to assault Kiev, the capital of Ukraine, just as the Germans were preparing to advance on Moscow.

The decision initially appeared to have been the right one, as the battle for Kiev, which began in late summer 1941, was quick and lasted less than two months. The Russians fought hard in defense, but they were bombarded by artillery, aircraft, and tanks and then encircled by the Germans. By the time the battle was over, approximately 600,000 Russian soldiers had lost their lives.

A Brutal Moscow Winter

When Hitler turned his attention back to the Russian capital, it was already November and the brutal Soviet winter had settled in. The decision to divert German troops to Kiev had given the Soviets much-needed time to reinforce Moscow's defenses, and Russian General Georgy Zhukov, a skillful tactician and respected leader, rallied his troops.

In spite of the fact that the Nazi supply lines had been disrupted and their troops were poorly equipped, the battle for Moscow initially ran in Germany's favor. Overcoming fierce Red Army resistance and breaching the three defensive lines the citizens of Moscow had built around the city, the Germans captured thousands of Soviet prisoners in an assault they dubbed Operation Typhoon.

In July 1942, German soldiers surrendered to the Red Army after a battle on the Russian Western Front.

During the winter of 1941–1942, Wehrmacht soldiers were not prepared for the frigid Russian weather.

When Russian general Zhukov mounted a counterattack in December, he used the extreme winter weather to his advantage. German troops were ill-prepared to fight in the harsh conditions and were sapped of the will to fight. By January 1942, Hitler's tactical error to take Kiev became obvious, as the Soviets broke through German lines and ended the attack against Moscow. Nazi units retreated, leaving behind thousands of tons of equipment.

German troops paid a terrible price for inadequate planning and poor choices. Germany was not defeated, but its military advances on the Russian capital had been stopped. For the next few years, while fierce battles continued to rage, Germany would slowly be pushed back, out of Russia.

The Caucasus

To continue its war effort, Germany needed oil, a vital resource that was abundant in the Russian Caucasus, a region that lay east of Turkey. Knowing how easily the German military had advanced through Yugoslavia and Greece, Hitler believed his troops could likewise sweep through the Balkans, conquer the Caucasus, and acquire the oil fields near the Black Sea.

In June 1942, one year after the launch of Operation Barbarossa, the initial attack on the Soviet Union, the Germans began Operation Blue with a twofold goal: to secure oil fields that were crucial to the Nazi war machine and to simultaneously deprive the Red Army of those same

In late 1941 and early 1942, Red Army troops came together in their fight to save Moscow. They continued to push the Germans away from the city.

In July 1942, a German infantry unit moved to the battlefront in the Ukraine.

resources, crippling Russia's ability to move equipment into battle.

Operation Blue started successfully, with the Red Army fighting, but losing very badly in southern portions of the Soviet Union. The initial triumphs buoyed the Germans who thought they had cleared an easy path to the Caucasus, and that from there, they could easily move north and continue to fight. In July 1942, despite his defeat in Moscow, Hitler told his generals that he believed that Russia was finished.

However, at that juncture, Hitler made a decision that changed the course of the war. He divided the advancing German army into two sections. Only one was to move on to the Caucasus; the other half was to engage the Red Army in the region west of the Don River near Stalingrad.

Hitler would not accept the surrender of Moscow; he wanted the city and its inhabitants utterly destroyed. These Soviet soldiers parading in Red Square went on to defeat the Germans.

General Georgy Zhukov, the "man who never lost a battle," lived up to his reputation during the fight for Moscow.

Red Army soldiers pushed the Germans back to Volokolamsk, about 75 miles west of Moscow.

German troops crossed the Don River in the Soviet Union using an improvised bridge. Despite the destruction, the soldiers pushed forward.

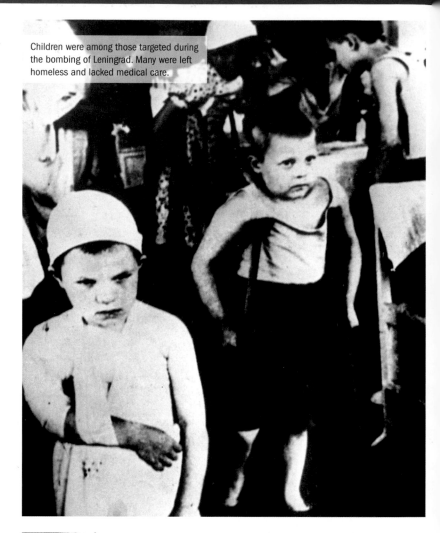

Children were among those targeted during the bombing of Leningrad. Many were left homeless and lacked medical care.

1942

Suffering in Leningrad

CIVILIANS WERE STILL TRAPPED, TRYING
TO SURVIVE HUNGER AND HARDSHIP.

During the winter months, the Nazi juggernaut sputtered. German troops who had seized Leningrad, north of Moscow, in 1941 were not prepared to fight a protracted battle or keep a city surrounded in the frigid cold of the 1941–1942 winter. Soldiers stole clothes from Russian peasants. Boots were in short supply, so Nazi soldiers sawed the legs off the dead and thawed them over fires so that they could remove and steal the corpses' footwear.

For the residents of Leningrad, life was equally harsh. Delivery of supplies was precarious and insufficient to help all those in need. Thousands died of starvation, others from the cold, but the citizens' resilience was profound. They would endure another two years of hardship before the siege finally ended in 1944.

Russians who died in Leningrad were transported to city cemeteries by grieving family members.

Residents of Leningrad had no potable water, so they gathered snow and ice from shell holes left by the German army.

German artillery continuously bombarded Leningrad, whose population was already suffering from starvation, disease, and subzero temperatures.

German soldiers barricaded themselves among heaps of rubble in the demolished neighborhoods of Stalingrad.

1942

Battle of Stalingrad

WITH LUCK AND CUNNING, THE RUSSIANS CRIPPLED THE ADVANCING GERMANS.

Stalingrad, a communications and industrial center that was home to many factories, was strategically located. Close to the Don River, it was the gateway to the oil-rich Caucasus region the Germans wanted. It was also on the Volga River, a major waterway used to ship grain. By seizing Stalingrad, the Germans believed that they could control the river and cut off major food supplies to Russia. In addition, they would be able to help themselves to the country's breadbasket, Ukraine.

Both sides knew that fighting for the metropolis would be fierce for symbolic reasons as well. The city's namesake, Joseph Stalin, was the leader of the Soviets and a hated enemy of the Germans. For the Nazis, taking the city would be a profound victory; for the Red Army, a humiliating loss. Both Hitler and Stalin had ordered that there would be no retreat, no surrender.

By late August, the Germans had advanced and reached the Volga. Led by Nazi General Friedrich Paulus, commander of the German Sixth Army, 250,000 to 300,000 troops began pounding Stalingrad with aerial bombings, artillery, and tanks. In September, German infantry and tanks stormed into Stalingrad, supported by the Luftwaffe.

Though troops were able to plant the Nazi flag in Red Square, they struggled once inside the city. Stalingrad's narrow, rubble-strewn streets proved difficult to navigate for German tanks designed for and accustomed to action in open rural spaces. What's more, the Germans were unprepared for the sniper units stationed in bombed-out buildings and the sheer determination of the Red Army.

Soviet troops took cover wherever they could in the rubble-filled streets of Stalingrad.

On January 30, 1943, Hitler promoted General Friedrich Paulus to field marshal, expecting that he would never give up. Paulus surrendered the next day to spare his decimated troops. He was taken prisoner by the Soviets.

During the battle of Stalingrad, Germans captured factories, brickworks, and entire blocks of homes.

German tanks were formidable in open territory on the battlefront, but they were less useful in Stalingrad's city streets.

Soviet Counterattack

Stalin had appointed Zhukov to lead the Soviets and to direct the defense of Stalingrad. Zhukov had six armies, almost one million men, to defend the city and began to position his troops in a line of defense. He hoped to wear down the enemy as they fought their way through the city. Even though the Germans had raised their flag at Red Square, they had not conquered the city. Fierce hand-to-hand combat,

supported by aerial attacks from the Luftwaffe, took place on the streets. Germans captured one portion of the city during the day; the Russians took it back at night.

Zhukov's plan was to weaken the Germans and then launch a massive counterattack. To that end, the Red Army moved tons of supplies, ammunition, and thousands of soldiers east of the city, where they would be ready to strike at the proper

moment. On November 19, Zhukov ordered Soviet reserve units into battle. The Soviets called the counterattack Operation Uranus, and in addition to ground troops, they had about 13,000 guns, 894 tanks, and 1,150 aircraft ready for battle. Zhukov targeted the weakest link in the German lines— the area manned by inexperienced Romanian troops. His men overran the Romanian-held positions and captured 65,000 prisoners.

The Soviets used their tanks effectively as they advanced northwest of Stalingrad.

Heavily armed Soviet soldiers took up their battle positions with only one goal—to defeat the Germans.

Romanian soldiers captured by the Soviets near Stalingrad in late 1942 marched through the snow. Most would not survive.

Civilians from Stalingrad tried to escape the chaos and fighting in their battered city.

Launching coordinated movements from the north, south, and east, the Red Army surrounded Stalingrad. In fighting that was considered among the most brutal of the war, the Soviets trapped the German Sixth Army. German general Paulus pleaded with Hitler to allow his troops to retreat, but he refused, determined that the army would fight to the last man. Hitler promised to send reinforcements and supplies, but they never arrived.

The Russian winter again took its toll on the Nazis. Unlike the Soviets, German soldiers did not have proper clothing, and cut off with no links to the outside, they did not have enough food. The determined Soviet people made do with little as well. They ate rats and made soup from wallpaper glue.

By late winter, the Germans were beleaguered and had no means to continue the fight. All the German troops in Stalingrad had surrendered by February 2, 1943. Of the nearly 300,000 men under Paulus's command, about 150,000 were dead or dying, 35,000 retreated from the front, and 91,000 had been taken prisoner. Only a few thousand of those would survive and return to Germany at war's end.

Historians consider the Battle of Stalingrad a turning point of the war. Germany would continue to fight but slowly retreated from the Soviet Union.

Polish prisoners lined up at Buchenwald, one of the first and largest concentration camps on German soil. More than 56,000 male prisoners would die here.

Einsatzgruppen

Formed just before the invasion of the Soviet Union, the Einsatzgruppen, or mobile killing squads, consisted of four paramilitary units of SS and police personnel, whose sole mission was to "liquidate" Jews and other groups, such as Roma, homosexuals, and political enemies of the Nazi Party, in the Soviet Union. Sent along with the German troops, these units began to kill entire Jewish communities, as well as the mentally and physically handicapped, officials of the Soviet state, and members of the Communist Party. Their primary means of extermination included gas vans and shootings, and they often went straight into Jewish communities to carry out their gruesome tasks. Many scholars believe that the Einsatzgruppen was the first implementation of the "Final Solution."

The Final Solution

PUTTING HIS WORDS INTO ACTION, HITLER BEGAN THE ERADICATION OF EUROPE'S JEWS.

Hitler's war was not confined to the countries of Europe. He waged a monstrous war of genocide against civilians, and the Nazis committed the worst crimes against humanity known to man. Having risen to power by blaming Jews for Germany's economic and social problems, as chancellor, Hitler enacted laws that victimized and persecuted his political opponents, especially Germany's Jewish population.

Prior to the German invasion of the Soviet Union in 1941, the Nazis had already herded Jews into ghettos in Poland and opened concentration camps in Germany. Following the Soviet invasion of Poland, the Nazis began to murder entire communities of Jews at home and in occupied territories. When Jews were identified, they were shot or forced into gas chambers. This approach caused psychological problems for some of the killers, spurring the Nazis to devise a more horrific and systematic plan.

After the Wannsee Conference in Germany on January 20, 1942, the Nazis implemented the "Final Solution," a methodical and elaborate system that herded Jews and other groups of people to extermination camps, where they were imprisoned, tortured, and eventually killed. By the time the Allies liberated the camps in 1945, the Nazis had exterminated six million Jews, Roma, homosexuals, and others they deemed unacceptable to society.

In response to the 1942 murder and deportation of some 300,000 Jews from the Warsaw Ghetto, Jewish civilians staged a revolt in April 1943. The protesters were arrested by Nazi troops.

The crematorium area at Dachau was built in 1942. Approximately 28,000 people were killed at the camp, although the total number will never be known.

Heinrich Himmler

Born into a middle-class, Catholic family, Reich SS leader Heinrich Himmler (1900–1945) was Adolf Hitler's most willing executioner. Himmler joined the Nazi Party in 1923 and became a confidant of Hitler. Himmler rose quickly through the ranks, and in 1936, Hitler appointed him Reichsführer SS and Chief of German Police. By that time, Himmler had already opened the first concentration camp at Dachau and become the chief architect of genocide. Determined to create Aryan supremacy, he oversaw extermination methods that included gassings, shootings, and starvation. By July 1942, Himmler decided to begin murderous medical experiments at Auschwitz, all part of the "Final Solution."

Dachau

When first opened in 1933, Dachau was designed to hold about 5,000 opponents of the Nazi regime. The total imprisoned at the camp would exceed 188,000.

American soldiers paraded through London's city streets in 1942.

The Yanks Arrive in Britain

THE UNITED STATES QUICKLY MOBILIZED AND SENT HELP TO THE ALLIES.

The U.S. declaration of war meant that Britain and its allies were no longer fighting alone, and following Pearl Harbor, the Americans quickly mobilized their military forces. In less than a year, the army grew by about 1.5 million, the navy by about 300,000, and the marines by about 100,000. Over the war years, more than 350,000 women would also serve.

Near the end of January 1942, the first influx of U.S. troops arrived in Britain. Many British were wary of the Americans. More than 50,000 civilians had died in German air raids, and food was in short supply. U.S. soldiers were better paid than their English counterparts and could afford things the Brits could not. Most of the troops had never been to Britain; many British had never seen an American.

The U.S. War Department printed a pamphlet entitled "Instructions for American Servicemen in Britain." It emphasized that Americans and the British needed to work together to defeat Hitler. The booklet admonished soldiers not to show off. To illustrate that the British and Americans were on equal footing, it pointed out that the English didn't know how to make a good cup of coffee, while U.S. servicemen were unable to prepare a good cup of tea. By 1944, there would be 1.5 million American soldiers serving in Britain.

British and American servicemen took the occasional time-out to relax, enjoy a band, and dance.

Troops from the United States stood at attention during a military inspection in London held in early 1942.

U.S. soldiers hosted an American-style Thanksgiving Day dinner in November 1942 for children who had suffered during the Blitz.

Thousands of Allied soldiers died during the fierce fighting in Bataan; more would die on the way to Camp O'Donnell.

1942

Bataan Death March

THE JAPANESE FORCED THEIR CAPTIVES ON A
LETHAL TREK THROUGH THE PHILIPPINE JUNGLE.

While American troops were being sent to Europe as part of the "Europe first" strategy, others were fighting in the Pacific. Even as Pearl Harbor smoldered, the Japanese captured Guam, the Solomon Islands, and other nations.

Japan also set its sights on the nearby Philippine Islands, owned at the time by the United States. In December 1941, General Douglas MacArthur, commander of U.S. forces in the Pacific, believed his troops would be able to hold off a Japanese invasion of the Philippines until the arrival of the Pacific Fleet. But MacArthur had underestimated the strength of his enemy, and with the Pacific Fleet in shambles, the Japanese quickly moved in, isolating MacArthur and his forces around Manila.

On December 23, 1941, MacArthur withdrew to the Bataan Peninsula on the island of Luzon and to Corregidor Island. The troops on Bataan faced a Japanese onslaught and a four-month siege. American and Filipino forces, weakened by starvation and disease, gallantly defended the islands, but to no avail. In February 1942, President Franklin Roosevelt ordered MacArthur to evacuate to Australia and he left in March. The troops stationed at the military post at Bataan surrendered on April 9. The Japanese captured about 75,000 troops, and the death march began the next day.

The Japanese forced the sick and malnourished prisoners to trek over 60 miles to a prison camp, killing many who lagged behind. Many prisoners died of hunger or starvation, while others were beaten to death. Between 7,000 and 10,000 men died during the brutal journey. The survivors, especially those held at Camp O'Donnell on Bataan, were kept with little food or water, and the death rate has been estimated at 400 per day.

Maltreated and severely punished, Americans and Filipinos had to march or die.

Japanese forces pulled down the American flag at Corregidor in May 1942.

Japanese general Waji-Ehk came to Manila, where he gave a radio broadcast about the fall of Bataan.

The Japanese aircraft carrier *Shōhō* was attacked by American bombers on May 7, 1942, during the Battle of the Coral Sea. After being hit by torpedoes, the ship sank within five minutes, taking most of her crew down.

1942

Coral Sea: The Route to Australia

AN AMERICAN VICTORY IN THE PACIFIC, THIS BATTLE MARKED A CHANGE IN THE WAR'S MOMENTUM.

By spring 1942, it appeared that the Japanese were unstoppable. They had conquered the Philippines, Burma, Malaya, and the Dutch East Indies with little resistance. This string of victories finally ended in May at the Battle of the Coral Sea.

The Japanese were moving quickly through the Pacific and planned to seize control of the Coral Sea, located between Australia and New Caledonia. They intended to invade Port Moresby in southeastern New Guinea. If the Japanese met with success there, Australia would be isolated and open to attack.

Prior to the battle, the Americans had cracked the Japanese naval code and learned of the plans. In response, the United States sent all available sea and air power to the region. On the morning of May 7, American and Japanese carrier groups faced off in the Coral Sea, but the ships actually never saw each other. It was instead a battle in the sky. American planes sank the Japanese carrier *Shōhō*, while the Japanese sank a U.S. destroyer and another vessel.

The battle spilled over into May 8. The Japanese sank the U.S. aircraft carrier USS *Lexington* and heavily damaged the USS *Yorktown*. If not completely victorious, the Americans had at least prevented the invasion of Port Moresby. While the Battle of the Coral Sea was considered a military draw, for the Allies, it represented a strategic victory. An even more important win was soon to come in the next great Pacific battle—Midway.

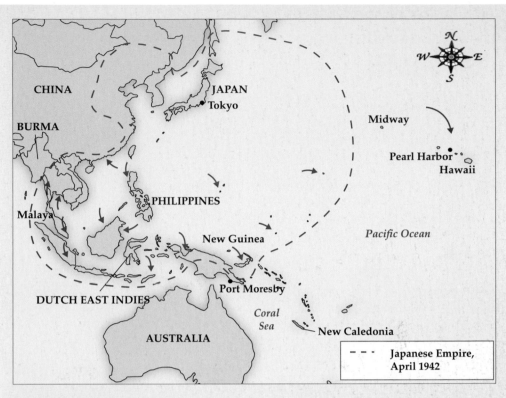

Island to Island, and Then to Australia

In 1942, Japanese forces were on the move through the islands in the Pacific. Capturing Australia and New Zealand seemed possible.

Not long after the USS *Lexington* was hit by Japanese torpedoes during the Battle of the Coral Sea, there was a giant explosion on the ship. It then caught fire and sank.

The *Lexington* was lost, but most of its crew, about 92 percent, was saved.

1942

Midway: Atoll in the Pacific

AFTER THE BATTLE OF THE CORAL SEA,
JAPANESE AND AMERICAN FORCES
CONTINUED TO STRUGGLE FOR DOMINANCE.

While the Americans may not have won a decisive battle in the air at Coral Sea, they put the Japanese on notice that U.S. ships and planes could fight and win. For their part, the Japanese were intent on establishing a central Pacific perimeter from which they could challenge American offensive actions.

As part of that plan, Japanese Admiral Isoroku Yamamoto, the mastermind behind the attack on Pearl Harbor, set his sights on a tiny but crucial atoll in the central Pacific. Midway, located about 1,300 miles northwest of Hawaii, was just a speck of land in a huge sea defended by a handful of U.S. servicemen. It was also home to an American naval base that was vital to Hawaii's safety. Yamamoto, in the waning days of May, initiated a scheme to draw out the remaining American aircraft carriers that had survived Pearl Harbor and to destroy them. By seizing Midway, he also hoped to force American defenses back to California and the Pacific Coast. Yamamoto, who had more ships at his disposal than the Americans, dispatched most of his fleet into battle with clear orders: Officers were to annihilate the American fleet and then to invade and occupy Midway.

But Yamamoto underestimated his American counterpart, Admiral Chester Nimitz, who had been named commander of the Pacific Fleet after Pearl Harbor and who had directed American operations in the Battle of the Coral Sea. Yamamoto conceived his plan thinking the Pacific Fleet would have only two carriers

Even though the U.S. lost the USS *Yorktown* to Japanese bombs and torpedoes, Midway, a tiny atoll in the Central Pacific, was ultimately an American victory.

Japanese Admiral Isoroku Yamamoto received a medal honoring his military efforts.

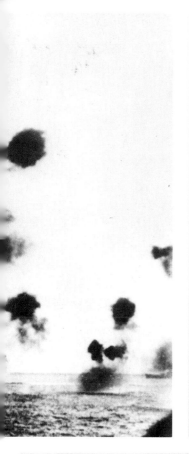

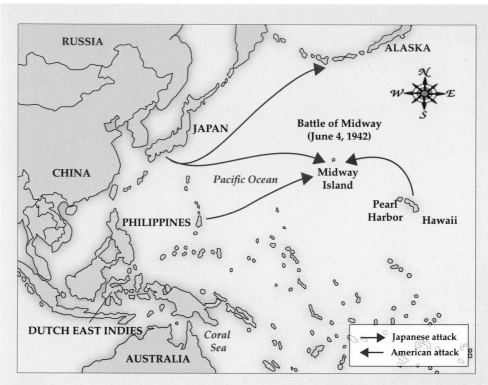

Midway
The tiny island lay about 1,300 miles from Honolulu and just over 2,500 miles from Tokyo.

A U.S. destroyer came to the aid of the USS *Yorktown*, but on June 7, two days after the ship was hit at Midway, it sank.

A squadron of torpedo bombers stationed on the USS *Enterprise* prepared to take flight during the Battle of Midway in June 1942.

available to defend Midway. In reality, a third battleship, the USS *Yorktown*, was also deployed. What's more, U.S. intelligence had learned of the plans for Midway, and the American fleet was ready to seek revenge for the losses at Pearl Harbor. Two Allied task forces gathered together on June 2 with orders to ambush Yamamoto and his fleet.

As with so many events in the war, luck played a role in the battle's outcome. Although the Americans knew that Japanese were steaming toward Midway, they did not know exactly where Yamamoto's fleet was and sent out plane after plane to locate it.

Finally, a seaplane flying out from Midway spotted the main

Japanese armada. By June 3, the Americans moved some 200 miles north of Midway and lay in wait for the Japanese fleet. Just after 4:00 a.m. on June 4, 108 Japanese planes attacked Midway, inflicting significant damage. Soon after, American dive-bombers retaliated. Their first attempts were futile, resulting in the loss of some

The *Kaga*, Japan's first heavy aircraft carrier, and one that had played a key role at Pearl Harbor, was sunk in the Battle of Midway, when it was hit by about 30 U.S. dive-bombers.

The U.S. naval base on Midway suffered heavy damage during the Japanese barrage.

65 aircraft. Yet, the Americans were tenacious and took full advantage of several Japanese blunders, including the mistaken perception that only a token U.S. force was nearby. Before the Japanese could respond to new intelligence, American planes pounced on the Japanese aircraft carriers *Akagi*, *Soryu*, and *Kaga*. The *Akagi*

exploded in a massive firestorm. Soon, the other Japanese carriers burst into flames.

Although the Japanese sank the carrier *Lexington*, the loss did not change the battle's outcome. Deprived of air cover, Japanese ships at the end of the day retreated and Yamamoto's task force slowly limped back to Japan.

While 307 U.S. servicemen died at the Battle of Midway, Japan sacrificed 322 aircraft and 3,500 men, and its navy would never recover from the losses. Following this American victory, Japan's navy was on the defensive. The momentum in the Pacific War, which had gone so badly for the Americans, had now swung to the United States.

1942

Moving through the Pacific

ALTHOUGH THEY WERE MOVING TOWARD JAPAN, ALLIED FORCES HAD TO BATTLE THEIR WAY THROUGH, ISLAND BY ISLAND.

The victory at Midway bolstered American confidence, and over the next four years, the United States committed itself to pushing the Japanese back to their homeland. To achieve this goal, MacArthur and Nimitz devised a strategy called "island hopping," where Americans captured and took control of one small isle after another in order to come within striking distance of the main Japanese islands.

Solomon Islands Campaign (1942–1945)

The first stage of the strategy began in the Solomon Islands, where the Japanese used the shipping lanes to ferry supplies and troops. Here, Allied troops fought a battle of attrition, wearing down the Japanese and inflicting massive losses.

Guadalcanal (August 1942–February 1943)

In June 1942, the Japanese built an air base on the island, threatening Allied movement in the region. On August 7, 6,000 U.S. Marines came ashore, surprised the Japanese, and seized the airfield. The Americans sent in reinforcements, and by January 1943, 44,000 troops were on the island. The bloody battle—a complex series of air, ground, and naval assaults—lasted until February. When it was over, the Japanese had lost roughly 10,000 soldiers, while the marines had lost about 2,000.

New Georgia (1942–1943)

In the fall of 1942, the Japanese occupied New Georgia, located in the middle of the Solomon Islands. By spring 1943, the U.S. launched Operation Toenail to dislodge the enemy. The battle was chaotic. Heavy rains reduced visibility; high winds and rough seas pummeled the invasion force. By August, the Japanese had retreated, although the Americans suffered significant losses.

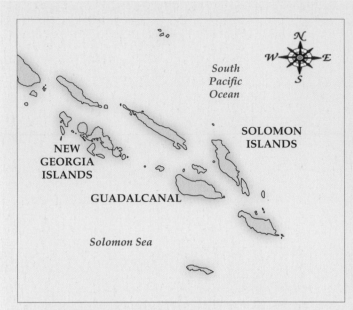

Island Hopping through the Pacific
U.S. forces moved from one island to another en route to Japan.

Marines came ashore on Guadalcanal prepared for battle.

Japanese soldiers were taken prisoner during the fighting at Guadalcanal, where brutal battles took place in the air, on land, and at sea.

Wounded soldiers on New Georgia Island were evacuated by any means possible.

In the pitched battle at El Alamein, a German tank was captured, and British troops, with bayonets drawn, took the crew prisoner.

1942

El Alamein: The Path to the Suez Canal

TWO GENERALS PITTED THEIR FORCES AGAINST EACH OTHER IN NORTH AFRICA IN AN EPIC 22-DAY FIGHT.

For three years, Allied and Axis powers had been fighting in the harsh terrain of North Africa. In the summers, they dealt with sandstorms; in the winter, mud bogged down troops and machines. German Commander Erwin Rommel had gained fame for his audacious tactics and victories in the desert. In January, he pushed eastward from Libya to Egypt in an attempt to seize the Suez Canal. The loss of the canal would leave the Allied supply route in tatters, and it would deliver a severe psychological blow to the British. The Allies were able to hold the Afrika Korps off until May, but German forces then advanced east to El Alamein, a city on the coast of Egypt about 150 miles from Cairo. In July, Rommel attacked, but the British counterattacked and managed to stave off the German advance.

Rommel was determined to push on, and this time, he would meet his match in British General Bernard Montgomery at the second battle of El Alamein. Montgomery had spent months reorganizing and resupplying his army. He was equipped with 300 new American-made Sherman tanks and over 200,000 troops. When he was ready, Montgomery picked the perfect place to fight—a 30-mile gap between the Mediterranean and the Qattara Depression, an area of salt marshes where Rommel's tanks couldn't operate.

The British attack began on October 23 with a blitz of artillery from 800 guns. After 10 days of nonstop battle, the Afrika Korps' troops, who had numbered about 100,000 at the beginning of the battle, were exhausted. Many were stricken with dysentery and dehydration. Tanks and armored vehicles needed repair, and supplies ran low.

On November 4, Rommel ordered his forces to retreat, and two days later, the British had driven the Germans west back into Libya. The Nazis lost more than 30,000 soldiers, killed, wounded, or captured. The battle had changed the war in favor of the Allies, and the Suez Canal remained in Allied hands for the rest of the war.

British Crusader and American Sherman tanks played a pivotal role in defeating the Germans.

German Commander Erwin Rommel, standing in the front, joined the crew of the 15th Panzer Division. During the battle, the Germans lost nearly 200 tanks.

British General Bernard Montgomery ("Monty") watched as the Germans retreated from El Alamein.

M4 Sherman Tank

When the American military realized it would play a role in the war, it placed an order for a new tank and was given the M3 Lee medium tank, named after the Civil War general Robert E. Lee. Manufacturers hurried the Lee into production and then rushed it to British armies fighting in North Africa in 1941.

A Short Life

The Lee was to have a short life. Retired in early 1942, it was soon replaced by the M4 Sherman, also named for a famous Civil War general, William Tecumseh Sherman.

This model would be redesigned multiple times as the war progressed. The earliest Sherman M4s were inspired by the German blitzkrieg and sacrificed heavy armor and firepower for speed. These tanks were immediately outclassed on the battlefield, where German vehicles boasted some of the best guns, optics, and armor in the European theater.

A Tank That Could Swim

By the time of the D-Day invasion, the M4 Shermans had been fitted with canvas sides, propellers, and large air intakes so that they could "swim" ashore. Weeks later, a variant dubbed the "hedgehog" added welded-on metal "teeth" to the front of the tank, allowing it to demolish the dense Normandy hedgerows. Another version had two long arms holding a spinning drum with whirring chains that beat the ground in front of the tank, safely detonating hidden mines.

Shermans advanced on the battlefield.

6 THE TIDE OF WAR TURNS

1943: THE ALLIED OFFENSIVE GAINED MOMENTUM WITH DECISIVE GAINS IN THE PACIFIC AND ITALY, WHILE THE GERMANS SUFFERED SETBACKS IN EASTERN EUROPE AND NORTH AFRICA.

On November 4, 1943, American troops trained for the invasion of Europe. What began with the Allied assault in Sicily would culminate with the landing at Normandy, D-Day, June 6, 1944.

"The massed, angered forces of common humanity are on the march. They are going forward—on the Russian Front, in the vast Pacific area, and into Europe—converging upon their ultimate objectives: Berlin and Tokyo."

—Franklin D. Roosevelt, July 28, 1943

After capturing enemy strongholds on Guadalcanal in early 1943, American troops helped sick and starving Japanese soldiers down to the beach.

"Guadalcanal . . . is the name of the graveyard of the Japanese army."

—Major General Kiyotake Kawaguchi

1943

American Victory at Guadalcanal

IN THIS TRIUMPH OVER JAPAN, U.S. TROOPS SECURED SEA LANES FROM AMERICA TO AUSTRALIA.

In the wake of the December 1941 attack on Pearl Harbor, the first U.S. offensive move against the Japanese took place at Guadalcanal, an island in the southwestern Pacific. American forces landed in August 1942, initiating a bloody, six-month-long confrontation between the two sides. As the battle wore on, both the United States and Japan committed extra troops, but by mid-January 1943, the U.S., with 44,000 soldiers, significantly outnumbered the Japanese.

On February 3, the U.S. succeeded in taking control of Guadalcanal. About 12,000 Japanese, many of whom were ill and malnourished, boarded waiting destroyers. The Americans had suffered losses as well, but with victories at Guadalcanal and Midway, the Allies were beginning to win against determined enemy forces.

Americans seized the Japanese flag that had flown over the airbase at Guadalcanal and held it for all to see.

The Axis Forces Weaken

In 1943, the Allies won battle after battle, but at a high cost for both sides.

1943
JAN

JANUARY 24 By the end of the Casablanca Conference, the Allies had established their end-of-war strategy.

FEB

FEBRUARY 2 What remained of the German Sixth Army surrendered at Stalingrad.

MAR

MARCH 13 The Nazis liquidated the Jewish ghetto at Kraków.

MAY 13 Axis forces in Tunisia surrendered, ending the North African campaign.

MAY

JULY

JULY 5 Battle of Kursk began, putting Germany on the defensive on the Eastern Front.
JULY 10 The Allies invaded Sicily, their first entry into western Europe.
JULY 25 Mussolini was deposed, and a new Italian government was formed.

1943

The Savage Battle of Tarawa

AT BETIO, IN THE CENTRAL PACIFIC, TOO MANY
AMERICAN SERVICEMEN FELL IN A MERE 76 HOURS.

The Americans were making headway in the Pacific theater, but the war there was still a bloody slog. No campaign underscored this more than the Battle of Tarawa. Located in the Gilbert Islands, about 2,500 miles southwest of Hawaii, Tarawa was a series of atolls nestled in protective beds of coral. The Japanese had seized the island chain in 1941 and reinforced Tarawa with mines, concrete fortifications, bunkers, and artillery. The largest of the islets was Betio, a half-mile-wide swath of coral,

where Japanese troops had dug in to protect an airstrip.

On November 20, the marines arrived in Betio but suffered heavy casualties, as the first landing craft were forced to drop their men hundreds of yards from shore. The marines waded in waist-deep water, stepping over sharp coral, directly into the line of fire. Those who made it to shore could not move up the beach. Determined and well-armed Japanese forces held their own positions, preventing an American advance.

Buoyed the next day by reinforcements, tanks, and artillery, the surviving marines broke out from the beachhead and stormed the enemy's barricades. The fighting continued for two days, and when it was over, only 17 of close to 4,700 Japanese survived. On the U.S. side, about 1,000 of 18,000 marines died, and another 2,000 were wounded, prompting some critics to question the value of taking such a small atoll. But the victory put the Allies on the edge of the western Pacific, closer to the Japanese homeland.

In November, U.S. marines towed comrades wounded at Tarawa toward help.

The conquest of Tarawa resulted in high casualties and adverse publicity, but Americans learned a lot about amphibious assaults.

Funerals for U.S. marines killed at Tarawa led to newspaper headlines such as "The Bloody Beaches of Tarawa."

Nearly as many Americans fell at Tarawa in 76 hours as were lost at Guadalcanal in six months.

A German U-boat disappeared under the waves after being rammed by a British destroyer.

1943

Conflicts Continue in the Atlantic

EVERYTHING ON LAND, SEA, AND AIR DEPENDED ON THE OUTCOME OF THIS LONG, HARD-FOUGHT DUEL.

The Battle of the Atlantic, one of the longest of World War II, was a high-toll struggle for Britain's survival. From the beginning of the war through the defeat of the Nazi Reich, the island nation fought to safeguard shipping lanes so that Allied merchant vessels could cross the ocean with food, equipment, oil, weapons, and other cargo. In all, about 3,000 Allied ships were destroyed by the Germans during the conflict and tens of thousands of men lost their lives.

As they had done in World War I, German submarines, also known as U-boats, hunted their prey in "wolf packs." They used a new type of radio transmitter to stalk the merchant ships, which were slow and had little means to protect themselves. Once an Allied convoy was identified, the U-boat would alert its sister ships who would converge, then wait until nighttime to attack.

In just six months in 1942, U-boats had sunk more than 500 merchant ships, and in early 1943, German U-boats were going about their deadly business virtually unscathed, and the German navy had increased the number of U-boats to over 500. March 1943, in particular, was an excellent month for the Germans as their submarines sank more than 20 escorted Allied merchant ships in the Atlantic. For Britain, which was running low on fuel, the Nazis' continued success constituted a crisis.

Finally, during April and May 1943, the Allies began making headway stemming the devastation. They increased the number of escort ships per convoy, produced new destroyers, and dispatched new planes to aid in the detection and destruction of U-boats. In those two months alone, the Allies blew up 45 U-boats and German shipyards were unable to produce replacements fast enough to make up for the losses. Though the battle in the Atlantic would continue, the tide was turning against the Nazis.

U-boats had to surface occasionally, and even the crews came up for fresh air.

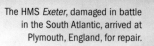

The HMS *Exeter*, damaged in battle in the South Atlantic, arrived at Plymouth, England, for repair.

Called "Operation Gomorrah," the joint British-American attack on Hamburg created an apocalyptic scene.

"If you can't hit the works, hit the workers."

—Arthur T. "Bomber" Harris

Hamburg

Since its founding in 825 near the Elbe River, Hamburg had long relied on shipping and trade to fuel its growth. The city's economy was so strong in the early 1900s that it was referred to as Germany's gateway to the world. But the Allied carpet-bombing campaign devastated Hamburg, and when World War II ended in 1945, the city was barely able to feed its remaining inhabitants. Hamburg today is Germany's largest port, an important commercial center, and the second-most populous city in the country.

1943

The Allied Air Campaign Heats Up

AFTER HAMBURG WAS BOMBED, JOSEPH GOEBBELS FELT THAT GERMANY MIGHT HAVE TO SEEK PEACE.

While the Soviet Red Army was doing most of the fighting against the Nazis on the ground in Europe in 1943, Britain and the United States terrorized the Germans from the skies. One of the deadliest campaigns occurred in July of that year when Allied planes, led by the British Royal Air Force, carpet bombed Hamburg, an industrial city near the North Sea with a population of nearly two million people.

The assault began on July 24. Flying at night, more than 700 RAF planes dropped thousands of tons of high explosives. The next day, American aircraft weighed in with bombs targeting Hamburg's military sites.

A successive raid conducted on July 28 created even more damage, setting off a firestorm that destroyed nearly half of the city.

In two weeks of bombings, the Americans and British lost a multitude of planes and men, but the numbers were nowhere near losses sustained by the Nazis. Over 40,000 Germans were killed, 30,000 were wounded, and about one million people were left homeless.

As the year ended, the Allies stepped up the aerial bombing campaign, targeting Berlin and other major cities. Long-range fighters, including the American P-51 Mustang, made such sorties deep into Third Reich territory possible.

The British hoped that the destruction of Hamburg would force Germany to end the war.

A woman and child wandered among the ruins of Hamburg after the July bombings. Until the air raids began, most German civilians had believed their country was winning the war.

A Boeing B-17 Flying Fortress took off for its mission to destroy German industrial sites.

Nearly 9,000 B-17s were produced in 1943 alone, mostly by women who replaced men in the U.S. workforce.

The Flying Fortress

Perhaps no one weapon symbolized the industrial might that the United States brought to World War II more than the B-17 Flying Fortress. The plane went from design to flight test in just under a year. The B-17 was a four-engine behemoth, armed with nine to 13 machine guns, including five .30-calibers, and the ability to carry an 8,000-pound bomb load.

The Flying Fortress saw action for the first time in 1941 when the RAF flew the plane during high-altitude bombing missions.

A U.S. ground crewman directed a P-51 Mustang fighter prior to takeoff. The P-51s escorted bombers, carried out strafing runs, and they were used in reconnaissance.

On October 17, 1943, the factory area in Schweinfurt was covered with smoke from fires and bursting bombs.

Curtis LeMay

Curtis LeMay (1906–1990) was a gruff, cigar-chomping U.S. Air Force general, an icon who flew as a copilot on the mission to destroy an airplane factory in Regensburg. LeMay was responsible for bringing the B-17s to England and pioneered the daylight bombing raids that devastated German factories, rail yards, and cities.

1943

Double Targets: Schweinfurt and Regensburg

THE GOAL OF THE DARING MISSION WAS TO CRIPPLE GERMANY'S AIRCRAFT INDUSTRY.

In the summer of 1943, Schweinfurt and Regensburg, two medium-sized factory towns in Bavaria, were targeted for bombing attacks by the Allies for a very simple reason: Their destruction could cripple Germany's ability to resupply its war machine.

Schweinfurt, just 100 miles east of Frankfurt, was home to five factories that produced ball bearings, small but essential components without which German tanks would not roll and airplane engines would not run. Regensburg, about 80 miles north of Munich, boasted a Messerschmitt airplane factory and an oil refinery. The Allied strategy was to reduce both cities to rubble.

The dual raid, flown by B-17s, would be the deepest into German territory that the planes had ventured, and they did so mostly alone, without a fighter escort. Military planners chose to hit Schweinfurt and Regensburg almost simultaneously on August 17.

On August 17, 1943, American B-17s attacked the aircraft factory at Regensburg that produced the Messerschmitt 109G, Germany's main fighter plane.

American pilots received a blessing before leaving for Germany. The bomber crews, usually consisting of 10 men, often suffered heavy losses.

A young U.S. airman waved from a B-17 Flying Fortress. Each crew member was trained for a specific mission task.

In Schweinfurt, the mission was large-scale, involving 400 B-17s. The planes reached their target in the afternoon and despite complications involving bombing accuracy, hell rained down on the town. Albert Speer, the Nazi armament minister, estimated that the raid resulted in a 38 percent drop in Germany's ball-bearing production.

In Regensburg, the Allies began releasing bombs at 11:43 a.m. While doing little damage to the town itself, the attacks decimated the main aircraft factory buildings and 37 newly made Messerschmitt 109s.

The Allies returned to Schweinfurt in October. This time, the B-17s destroyed about two-thirds of Schweinfurt's production capacity.

Though the Schweinfurt and Regensburg mission was labeled a success, it was a costly one. The B-17s flew in tight formations, which made them easy targets for antiaircraft fire. About 120 Allied bombers were shot down, and more were damaged during these raids. More than 600 Americans were either captured or lost in the battles, a very high 20 percent casualty rate.

Workers assembled Messerschmitts in this Augsburg, Germany, plant. The fighter lacked the long-range capability of the U.S. P-51 Mustang.

The B-17s flew into heavy German flak as they dropped their bombs over Schweinfurt, resulting in heavy American losses.

1943

Targeting North Africa

DESPITE FIELD MARSHAL ERWIN ROMMEL'S BEST EFFORTS, HE COULD NOT WIN IN NORTH AFRICA WITHOUT SUPPLIES.

Allied forces had begun winning battles in Europe and the Pacific, and they were slowly gaining an upper hand in North Africa as well. But Allied leaders, especially Prime Minister Winston Churchill and President Franklin Roosevelt, disagreed on whether to continue with a focus on North Africa or to begin an invasion of Europe.

Roosevelt sided with Soviet Premier Joseph Stalin, who was urging the Allies to open a new front in Europe to help relieve the pressure on the Eastern Front. Churchill, in contrast, was intent on protecting British interests in North Africa. He was convinced the Allies could repeat their initial success of 1942, when they forced Germans to retreat from conquered territories in Egypt. In the end, Churchill prevailed. The result was Operation Torch, launched in November 1942.

Fighting in North Africa was fierce, with losses and victories on both sides. Although some 65,000 Allied troops participated in Operation Torch, the pace of the advance was slower than expected. The terrain was harsh and the Germans were determined to fight.

Initially, Nazi resolve helped buoy the army and their troops achieved some successes. But by the spring of 1943, those victories began to be overshadowed by successive catastrophes.

Allied air forces and navies wrested control of the Mediterranean Sea, thereby shutting down transport routes between Sicily and North Africa. Nazis and Italians were forced to bring in supplies and reinforcements by air, efforts which proved disastrous. At the same time, the Axis feared losing Tunisia, which would leave Sicily and the Italian boot open to invasion.

Allied forces advanced into Tunisia, where they cut Field Marshal Erwin Rommel's forces from their supply bases. Axis troops were trapped in a pocket along the Tunisian coast.

Pursued by the Eighth Army after the fall of Tripoli, German troops retreated to the frontiers of Tunisia.

A British soldier searched a German captured near Sedjenane in Tunisia. Large numbers of Axis soldiers were apprehended and sent to prisoner-of-war camps.

British General Montgomery (center) played a key role in the battlegrounds of North Africa and Europe.

1943
A Stunning About-Face

AFTER A DECISIVE VICTORY IN TUNISIA, THE AFRIKA KORPS WAS FORCED INTO RETREAT BY BRITISH GENERAL MONTGOMERY.

In 1941, Hitler told Benito Mussolini to fight harder in North Africa. A year later, Mussolini warned Hitler, who had paid little attention to what was happening in the region, that an Axis defeat in Tunisia might mean Allied control of the Mediterranean and a subsequent invasion of Italy. The German leader responded by announcing that Tunisia was "the cornerstone of our conduct of the war on the southern flank of Europe" and ordered that the country be held at all costs.

Hoping to wear down Allies who had landed troops in French-held North Africa in late 1942, the Germans began building up their defenses. Field Marshal Erwin Rommel's first goal was to hold onto territory that the Italians had gained in the area, and in February 1943, his forces launched an offensive against Allied lines in Tunisia. Rommel attacked at the weakest point in the Allied lines—the Kasserine Pass, a two-mile gap in the Dorsal Mountains, which was defended by the Americans.

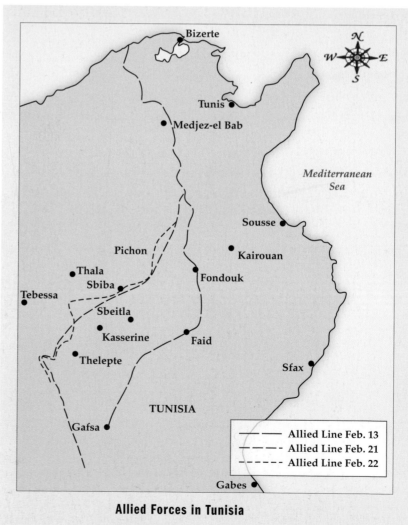

Allied Forces in Tunisia

"In a man-to-man fight, the winner is he who has one more round in his magazine."

—Erwin Rommel

Rommel with his troops on the Tunisian front in March 1943

On June 8, 1943, Allied leaders met in Algiers, with Churchill (middle) presiding. Attendees included British Foreign Secretary Anthony Eden (left), generals George C. Marshall, Dwight D. Eisenhower, and Bernard Montgomery (right). President Franklin Roosevelt, knowing the pressure that Churchill would apply to Eisenhower, sent Marshall, his chief of staff, to monitor the proceedings.

Debacle in the Desert for the Allies

The United States beat back the Germans' initial attacks at the Battle of Kasserine Pass, but the Afrika Korps quickly regrouped and repelled the Allies, primarily Americans, in this strategic battle. German Panzers and infantry overwhelmed the U.S. soldiers, many of whom panicked and fled, leaving behind almost all of their equipment. The Americans were pushed back 50 miles, and Allied forces lost 10,000 men, more than half of whom were U.S. servicemen.

The defeat was humiliating for the United States and caused great consternation among the ranks, while devastating morale back home. It also prompted General Dwight Eisenhower, who had control of troops in Europe and North Africa, to clean house. He unified troop command so that all Allied forces, soldiers, sailors, and aviators—who came from a number of countries— could fight as a coordinated unit. In addition, Eisenhower changed Allied leadership in North Africa, installing General George Patton, a master of tank warfare, in command of the U.S. Army II Corps. By March, Patton had counterattacked and regained the Americans' original positions.

The Mareth Line

Following the routing at Kasserine Pass, British General Bernard Montgomery prepared his troops to assault the Mareth Line, a natural defensive position that ran 22 miles

American troops drove along Jules Ferry Avenue in Tunis, Tunisia, after taking the city on May 5. Several weeks later, a parade celebrated the end of fighting in North Africa.

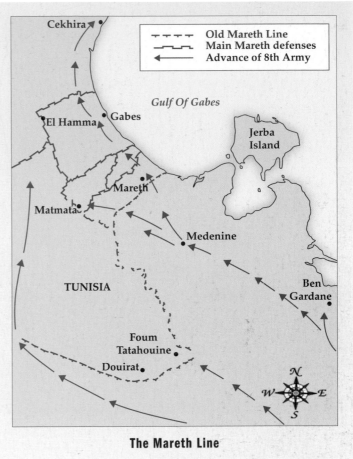

The Mareth Line

Dwight D. Eisenhower

General Eisenhower (1890–1969) served in the United States Army after he graduated from West Point Military Academy in 1915. Known for his organizational skills and his ability to work well with others, Eisenhower rose through the military ranks, and in 1942, he was given command of all American forces in Europe. He led Operation Torch and commanded the Allied forces in North Africa and then served as commander of the forces that invaded Sicily and Italy. The following year, Eisenhower served as supreme commander of the Allied troops who invaded France on D-Day, June 6, 1944; and in 1945, he was named U.S. Army chief of staff. In 1952, Eisenhower was elected to serve as the 34th president of the United States, an office he held for two terms.

from the Tunisian coast inland to the mountains that the French had fortified with a series of bunkers. The Mareth Line had been designed as a defense against Italy as it invaded North Africa. Instead, the Axis powers were planning to use it to defend against the British. Rommel had left North Africa in early March for health reasons, and General Hans-Jürgen von Arnim was put in charge.

Montgomery's plan was to tighten the noose around the remaining Axis troops while ensuring that they did not escape to Sicily. As Patton staged a diversion, Montgomery went on the offensive with armies that included troops from New Zealand and the Free French Forces. Over the next three months, Montgomery would take the Mareth Line and hold it, forcing the enemy to turn back. The defeated Axis

troops retreated and began to prepare for the final battle in Tunisia.

Montgomery's men met the British First Army south of Tunis for the push into the country's capital. Starting with a massive artillery bombardment, the attack was decisive. On May 7, the the British marched into the city, and within a week, the Axis forces in North Africa, about 250,000 Germans and Italians, surrendered.

"No amphibious attack in history had approached this one in size . . . there were hundreds of vessels and small boats afloat and ant-like files of advancing troops ashore."

—Dwight D. Eisenhower

In July, British soldiers raced ashore in Sicily. The landing helped prepare troops, who would soon storm the beaches of Normandy.

1943

Operation Husky: The Invasion of Sicily

THE ALLIES HOPED TO DIVERT GERMAN DIVISIONS FROM FRANCE AND CREATE ANOTHER FRONT IN EUROPE.

By the summer of 1943, the Allies had emerged as the victors in North Africa. They then agreed that their forces were ready to invade Europe from the south, through the Italian island of Sicily, in some points less than two miles from the mainland. Successfully occupying Italy would secure Mediterranean shipping lanes and would provide air bases from which to bomb the rest of southern Europe.

Eisenhower was given command of the overall operation, code-named Husky. More troops were involved than would be engaged in the D-Day invasion. Eisenhower deployed approximately 3,000 ships, 150,000 soldiers, and about 4,000 aircraft. Allied armies were split into two groups. The first, which was led by Britain's general Montgomery, was to land near Syracuse in southeastern Sicily and advance along the coast toward the port city of Messina. From there, the Allies could easily reach the Italian mainland. The second army, led by Patton, was to march across western Sicily, capture Palermo, and then drive east toward Messina.

The invasion began during the night of July 9–10 with a naval and air bombardment and the landing of airborne troops. The next day, the seaborne attack began in terrible weather. Enemy resistance along the coast was weak, and by nightfall, the large Allied force had secured the beaches. The British moved easily across the island and within three days, their forces occupied the southeastern part of Sicily.

In June, the island of Pantelleria, home to a German airfield, was wreathed in smoke from Allied bombardment.

American troops walked down a war-ravaged street in Messina, Sicily, on August 24.

On August 17, trucks loaded with thousands of Italian prisoners clogged the north coast roads of Sicily.

General George Patton stood on a beach during the campaign in Sicily. Often called "Old Blood and Guts" by his men, Patton was brave and tenacious, willing to go wherever the fighting was worst.

Italian prisoners of war waited patiently on the beach while their captors helped the wounded.

Race to Messina

American General Patton refused to give his British counterpart Montgomery the glory of capturing Messina. After reaching Palermo on the northwest coast on July 22, Patton and his troops took control of the city within just a few days—a victory that was followed by the ouster of Italy's fascist dictator Mussolini on the 25th. Patton then pushed his forces hard toward the east and Messina. "This is a horse race in which the prestige of the U.S. Army is at stake," Patton wrote to one of his commanders.

Though the Italians continued fighting, a crack had opened in the Rome-Berlin Axis. On August 11, German Field Marshal Albert Kesselring decided that Sicily could no longer be defended and ordered his troops to withdraw across the Straits of Messina to Italy. The Germans evacuated more than 39,000 troops and nearly 10,000 vehicles.

On August 17, 1943, Patton arrived in Messina hours ahead of the British. Seizing Sicily paved the way for the invasion of southern Europe. Still, Operation Husky did not come without a tremendous cost. Fighting claimed more than 12,000 British casualties and 8,781 Americans. The Germans suffered an estimated 29,000 casualties, and close to 140,000 Axis troops were taken prisoner.

In September 1943, Montgomery and Eisenhower studied the Italian mainland. They were making final preparations for the assault across the Straits of Messina.

On August 16, 1943, a Sicilian man offered wine to U.S. soldiers. When German Field Marshal Albert Kesselring ordered the evacuation of troops from Sicily, Italian forces had already begun to leave.

On July 12, 1943, these T-34 tanks of the Red Army advanced during the Battle of Prokhorovka at the Kursk Bulge, about 18 miles from the city of Belgorod. A total of 1,500 tanks were involved in this battle.

1943

Battle of Kursk

SOVIET AND BRITISH INTELLIGENCE LEARNED OF HITLER'S PLANS FOR OPERATION CITADEL, GIVING THE SOVIETS TIME TO PREPARE.

The city of Kursk, roughly 300 miles south of Moscow, straddled the Moscow-Rostov railway. By the spring of 1943, Kursk was also at the center of a buildup of Soviet troops, with soldiers stationed 150 miles north to south and pushing 100 miles west into the German lines. Hitler had already flown to the front to meet with Field Marshal Erich von Manstein to discuss what to do about the bulge and to plan for continuing German movements in the USSR. It was becoming increasingly clear that the Nazis would have to attack the Red Army north and south of Kursk.

Hitler decided to postpone this battle, called Operation Citadel, until the weather warmed. He wanted to make sure that Germany had the necessary armaments, that von Manstein was well supplied with Germany's new powerful Tiger tanks, and that the heavy tanks would not bog down in the winter mud.

On April 15, Hitler concluded that it was time for battle. "This offensive is of decisive importance," the Führer said. "It must end in swift and decisive success . . . Victory at Kursk will be a beacon for the whole world." It was to be a surprise attack, one that would destroy the Soviet forces.

The Soviets had received information from spies and the British about the Germans' plans, and the Red Army was prepared. By July, the Soviets had a distinct advantage. Red Army troops outnumbered the Germans at least two to one. More than 20,000 Soviet artillery pieces were in place, along with 6,000 tanks and several thousand airplanes. Russian civilians dug 3,000 miles of trenches to slow the impending German attack, and Russian soldiers placed well over 400,000 antitank and antipersonnel mines.

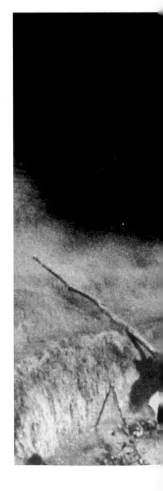

German Tiger tanks stopped near Kharkov in August. The Russians had planted so many mines that tanks did not advance easily.

The Soviets learned about Operation Citadel from German prisoners. This led to a preemptive, massive Soviet artillery bombardment early on July 5.

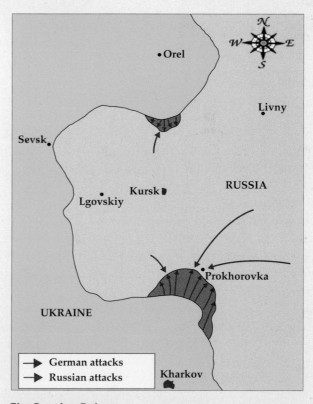

German attacks
Russian attacks

The Russian Bulge

Although the battle became known for Kursk, the city, located about 300 miles southwest of Moscow, was not the target.

A German Panzer VI tank made its way toward the Russian front, between Belgorod and Orel, on July 1, 1943. By mid-July, German forces had lost about two-thirds of their tanks.

Erich von Manstein
Promoted to field marshal in 1940, Erich von Manstein (1887–1973) was known as one of Germany's best military minds. He was respected for his strength of character; and while he did not always succeed, he was known for presenting his views to his superiors, including Hitler. After Hitler disastrously refused to let the Nazi army retreat from Stalingrad, von Manstein was able to argue successfully that he should regroup the German forces in Russia. At the end of the war, von Manstein stood trial for war crimes and was imprisoned until 1953. Following his release, he advised the German government on army affairs.

A Slow Start to a Terrible Battle

During the early morning hours of July 5, the greatest tank battle in history began. Two million men, 6,000 tanks, and 4,000 aircraft faced off against each other. Slowed by the mines and Soviet defenses, the Germans gained only six miles of territory within the first 24 hours, at a cost of 25,000 killed or wounded. Within the week, the Germans had advanced only 10 miles.

On July 12, the Soviets launched a counterattack coinciding with the Allied invasion of Sicily. By this time in 1943, Russian planes had improved and Allied air power had emerged as a dominant factor in the war. The slow-moving Panzer Tiger tanks were easy targets for the Red Army antitank guns, and the tanks were forced to hide in dense forests for protection during daylight hours. Even with its 88-mm gun, a Tiger could not hold its own against Soviet fire, and most tanks were disabled if hit on the side. At battle's end, the Soviets had destroyed nearly 70 percent of the German tanks, while Soviet tanks and aircraft wreaked havoc on the remaining Nazi forces.

Weakened by the Sicily invasion, the Germans were forced to abandon the Battle of Kursk, and by late July, the Red Army had pushed the Nazis west, back to their original position. The Nazi defeat was a major blow to the Third Reich and would be the last battle where Germany took the offensive in the East. Going forward, the Nazis would be on the defensive, trying to prevent the great Soviet missions that would follow in the next two years.

German tanks were on the move near Belgorod in July 1943. A few weeks later, they had lost the Battle of Kursk.

An exhausted German gunner was taken prisoner in the battle at the Kursk Bulge. German morale plummeted with the heavy losses of both men and matériel.

1943

The Resistance

UNDERGROUND MOVEMENTS FORMED
DURING THE WAR, AND THEY PLAYED A
VITAL ROLE IN HELPING DEFEAT GERMANY.

The Nazis dominated Europe, and citizens had no means of escape. Many did not acquiesce to Germany's policies nor to the brutal occupying forces. Resistance movements—secret armies of partisans—formed in most occupied countries.

France

The term *French Resistance* covered a number of groups in France who opposed both the Nazis in the north and the Vichy government in the south. Following the German invasion of the Soviet Union, Communist groups in France united and gained a reputation for serving as aggressive fighters. Others joined the movement to protest Nazi policies, particularly against the Jews. Collectively, the groups gathered intelligence for the Allies, destroyed communication lines, and helped escaped prisoners of war find a way to safety. It is estimated that about 40,000 French were involved in the resistance in 1943; by 1944, the number had jumped to 100,000.

Denmark

Denmark had been occupied by the Germans since 1940, but the Danes had retained some control over their government. However, in 1943, the Nazis seized total control, prompting a surge in acts of sabotage by partisans. The number of people participating in the resistance mushroomed quickly to about 20,000.

Belgium and the Netherlands

The Belgians and the Dutch had strong resistance movements. The Belgians were especially successful at passing intelligence

reports on to Britain. They also performed acts of sabotage to hinder the Germans, and they helped escaped prisoners of war. The Dutch had been outraged when the Nazis invaded their country, and they were horrified by the treatment of the Jewish population. They sent information to the Allies, including details about the German divisions that were in Arnhem in 1944, intelligence the Allies ignored with catastrophic consequences.

Yugoslavia

Two bands of fighters battled the Germans in Yugoslavia. The first was led by Josip Tito, an avowed Communist; the other was led by Draza Mihailovic, who supported Yugoslavia's royal family living in exile in London. Despite their differences, the two men at first formed a united front against the Nazis. But their political ideologies were so different they could not agree on any major points. By September 1941, Tito had raised an army of 70,000 resistance fighters who engaged in guerrilla warfare. Tito's fighters suffered many casualties, but Tito became a national hero. Mihailovic was charged with treason and collaborating with the Germans; in 1946, he was executed.

Soviet Union

Operating in western Belorussia between 1942 and 1944, a group of Jewish partisans were led by three brothers, Tuvia, Asael, and Zus Bielski. Spurred by the murder of their parents and two brothers, the Bielskis first fought to save their own lives but soon banded together to help save more than 1,200 Jews survive Nazi atrocities, and to fight to defeat the Germans.

In 1943, the Germans sent 20,000 military and police in a manhunt for this group of partisans. But under the Bielskis' leadership, they moved to the forest, where they established a mobile community complete with a mill, bakery, and laundry, and they worked with other Soviet partisans.

In October 1943, a Soviet partisan detachment was on the march. After the German attack on Russia, Communist groups began to form resistance movements to fight Nazi occupation.

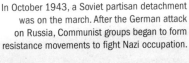

In November 1943, Josip Broz, then at the head of the Yugoslavian Communist Resistance Movement, was named marshal (under the name of Tito), commander of the Anti-Fascist Council of National Liberation.

A branch of the Yugoslav resistance stopped by the Sutjeska River valley as they tried to escape the Nazis.

The German cipher machine, code-named Enigma

Codes, Deception, and Spies

THE ALLIES DEVELOPED ESPIONAGE FORCES, CRITICAL FOR GATHERING AND DISPERSING INFORMATION.

Code-breakers, spies, and seized documents can sometimes turn the tide of a campaign. One of the biggest breakthroughs for the Allies was the capture of the Enigma machine and its codebooks, the means by which the Germans sent encrypted messages. Many have claimed that by securing the Enigma machine, the Allies shaved two years off the war, though others have suggested the coup had limited value because it took too long to get the decoded information to field commanders.

Operation Mincemeat

Few deceptions of the war were as successful as Operation Mincemeat. Determined to convince the Germans and Italians that the invasion of southern Europe was going to take place in Sardinia and Greece, not Sicily, British intelligence planned an elaborate ruse. They obtained a body from a London coroner, created a new identity for him, and chained a briefcase to his wrist. The briefcase contained bogus documents that pointed to the fake invasion. The body was taken by submarine and tossed overboard, discovered by Nazi spies off the coast of southern Spain in April 1943. The documents convinced Hitler to send troops to Greece and Sardinia, allowing the Allies to successfully invade Sicily while also bringing Mussolini's reign to an end.

Navajo Code Talkers

The Japanese were experts at breaking American codes. Then, a U.S. marine named Philip Johnston, the son of a missionary who had been raised on the Navajo reservation and one of the few non-Navajos who spoke their language, realized that if messages were transmitted in the Navajo language, the Japanese would never be able to decode them. The Navajos who sent and translated the messages were known as code talkers, and they participated in U.S. Marine assaults in the Pacific from 1942 until war's end, 1945.

Navajo cousins, Privates First Class Preston and Frank Toledo, relayed orders over a field radio in their native tongue at Ballarat, Australia, on July 7, 1943.

1943

The Conferences of 1943

CHURCHILL AND ROOSEVELT WORKED
WELL TOGETHER, DESPITE THEIR VERY
DIFFERENT PERSONALITIES.

Roosevelt and Churchill were forces of nature, partners thrown together by history, each well suited to leading their nations at war and directing the task of defeating the Axis powers. Over the course of the war, the two men forged a close working relationship. A few weeks after Pearl Harbor, Churchill traveled to Washington, DC, to meet with Roosevelt, in what historians now call the First Washington Conference. At the meeting, code-named "Arcadia," the two men agreed that the defeat of Germany should be paramount above other strategic objectives. In January 1943, two months after the successful invasion of North Africa, the two met again, this time in Casablanca, on the Moroccan coast.

At the Casablanca Conference, the Allied leaders finalized battle plans and boldly announced that they would accept nothing less than the unconditional surrender of the Axis. Roosevelt, however, clearly stated that unconditional surrender did not mean the annihilation of German, Japanese, and Italian populations, but the destruction of the philosophies in those countries which were based on conquest and the subjugation of other people.

At the end of 1943, Roosevelt and Churchill met again, this time in Tehran, Iran, with Stalin. As they had done at Casablanca, the leaders coordinated strategy, and Stalin continued to push for an invasion of France. Stalin also agreed to enter the war against Japan once Germany was defeated.

On December 22, 1941, Churchill and Roosevelt met at the White House in Washington, DC. During their meetings, the two leaders decided that their highest war priority would be the Atlantic theater and the defeat of Germany and Italy.

In January 1943, Roosevelt and Churchill met at Casablanca, where they decided to demand the unconditional surrender of the Axis powers. Premier Joseph Stalin was invited, but he was unable to attend.

Between November 28 and December 1, 1943, the "Big Three" (Stalin, Roosevelt, and Churchill) attended the Tehran Conference in Iran, where they organized their strategy for defeating the Axis powers and discussed postwar matters. The Americans committed to invading France in the spring of 1944, and Stalin agreed to declare war on Japan once Germany was defeated.

7 | OVERWHELMING FORCE

1944: THE ALLIES WON DECISIVE VICTORIES ON THE EASTERN FRONT IN EUROPE AND IN THE PACIFIC. THEY ALSO LAUNCHED MAJOR OFFENSIVE CAMPAIGNS ALONG THE WESTERN FRONT.

"You are about to embark on a great crusade . . . We will accept nothing less than full victory!"

—General Dwight D. Eisenhower

Omaha Beach, June 6, 1944

1944

Ending the Siege of Leningrad

MORE THAN ONE MILLION RUSSIANS DIED DURING THE 872-DAY CONFLICT, BUT THEY NEVER SURRENDERED.

The Axis powers invaded Russia in June 1941. Three months later, Leningrad was surrounded by German forces. Cut off from the rest of Russia, the city was left without resources, and food was rationed to two slices of bread per day.

In January 1943, the Russians were able to establish a land connection to Leningrad, dubbed Operation Iskra. That single eight-kilometer corridor across Lake Ladoga helped feed and supply a starving population, and though Leningrad was still surrounded by enemy forces, the road helped save the city from capture.

A year later, with the German Army Group North weakened, Russian forces finally pushed the Germans out of the southern side of Leningrad. When Reich Chancellor Adolf Hitler refused his generals' request to fall back to the Panther Line near the Baltic Sea, German troops were forced to await events on the Leningrad and Volkhov fronts.

Civilians joined Russian troops and took advantage of every chance they had to fire at their German opponents.

Dressed in winter camouflage, Soviet troops were prepared to advance against German lines.

Allies on the March

1944 was a year of hard-fought battles, optimism, and defeat for both Allied and Axis powers. But by the end of the year, it was clear that the Allies would prevail.

APRIL 4 General Charles de Gaulle took charge of French forces.

MAY Battle of Monte Cassino ended.

▲ **JUNE 5** Operation Overlord, the invasion of Normandy

JUNE 6 D-Day (see p. 184)

JUNE 22 Operation Bagration (see p. 190)

APRIL • • • • **MAY** • • • • **JUNE** • • • • • • • •

Well-armed Soviet troops opened fire at German soldiers just outside Leningrad.

SEPTEMBER Operation Market Garden (see p. 195)

OCTOBER Battle of Leyte Gulf (see p. 196)

NOVEMBER 12 Sinking of the *Tirpitz* (see p. 181)

▲ **DECEMBER** Bastogne, a key battle in the Ardennes

DECEMBER Battle of the Bulge (see p. 200)

SEPTEMBER · · · · · OCTOBER · · · · · NOVEMBER · · · · · DECEMBER

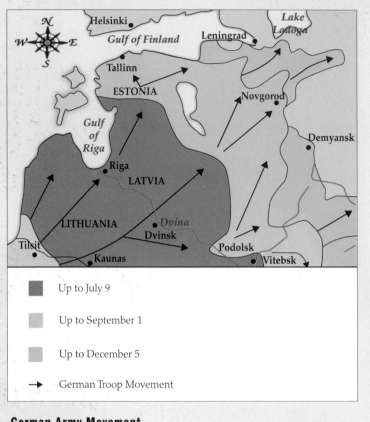

German Army Movement
German troops moved north through Lithuania and Latvia to reach Leningrad.

Legend:
- Up to July 9
- Up to September 1
- Up to December 5
- → German Troop Movement

The Ice Road that Saved Leningrad

During the siege, the only reliable way to bring supplies into Leningrad was via a road over Lake Ladoga; the road only worked when the lake was frozen, and it had to be frequently rebuilt. The Road of Life was also known as the Road of Death. The Germans made it a bombing target, and transport vehicles got bogged down in the snow, trapping them. Others fell through the ice, bringing the troops to a frigid death.

Operation January Thunder

General Leonid Govorov, the top Russian commander of the Leningrad front, planned "Operation January Thunder" to liberate the historic city from the Germans in 1944. The Russians began a bombardment from Oranienbaum (now called Lomonosov), about 30 miles from Leningrad. In the Krasnoye Selo-Ropsha Offensive, the Russians fired more than 100,000 shells in just over an hour.

A second, more intense attack followed the next day when more than 200,000 shells were fired. The Russians advanced quickly and broke through the German lines, forcing the Nazis to fall back to the Panther Line near the Baltic Sea.

The last German shell fell on Leningrad on January 23, and by the end of the month, the Germans had been pushed back more than 40 miles from their original position.

The Moscow-Leningrad railroad line was restored, and Premier Joseph Stalin declared the port city liberated.

The blockade of Leningrad, called the "900-day siege" by the Russians, actually lasted 872 days. When it was finally over, 3,200 residential buildings, 900 homes, and over 800 factories in the city and its suburbs had been destroyed. The once-thriving metropolis of about 3.5 million had roughly 700,000 survivors, and by most counts, several hundred thousand of those were soldiers who had come from other parts of Russia to help defend the city.

The Red Army continued its advance and mounted major offensives against the retreating Germans. The Soviets were working under the belief that if they kept up their fierce offensive, German defense lines would have to break.

Grieving families had to travel by foot to transport the deceased to cemeteries during the Leningrad blockade.

Soviet soldiers from the Volkhov and Leningrad fronts greeted each other jubilantly when their armies were reunited.

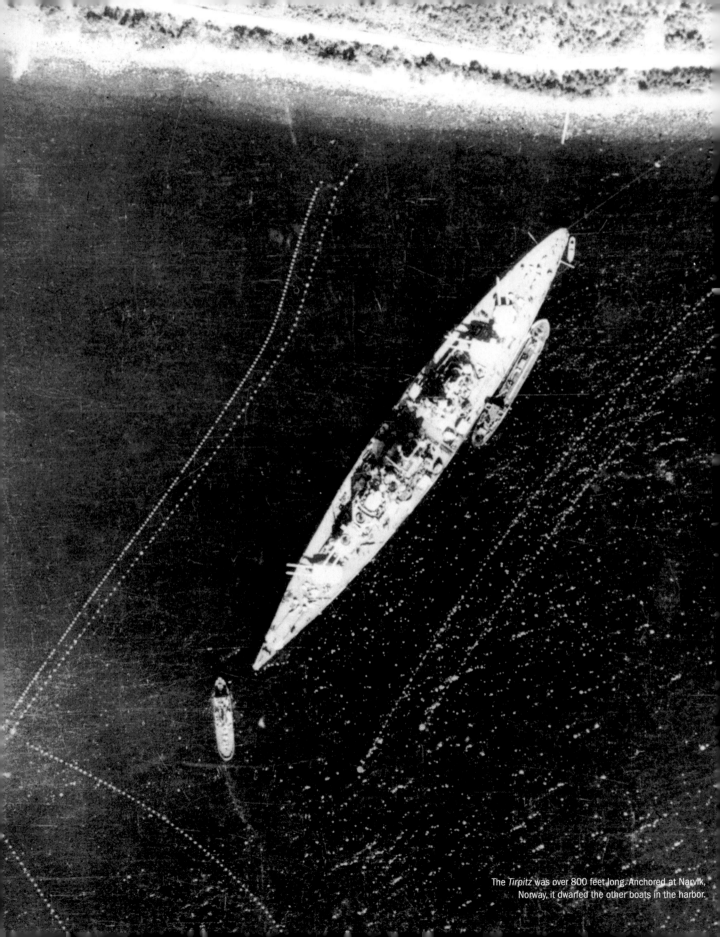

The *Tirpitz* was over 800 feet long. Anchored at Narvik, Norway, it dwarfed the other boats in the harbor.

1944

Blockades, Behemoths, and U-Boats

THE BATTLE IN THE NORTH ATLANTIC HEATED UP
AND ALLIES USED RADAR TO THEIR ADVANTAGE.

▲ On the left, the *Tirpitz* hit by British bombers; in the center, the sunken *Tirpitz*; on the right, in 1949, German and British ships tried to raise the ship.

To deny the German war machine the resources it needed and to prevent the German navy from resupplying its fleet, the Allies had begun a blockade in the North Atlantic not long after the war began. Among other strategies, the Allies mined northern harbors used by Germany, cutting off shipments of critical war matériel.

By 1944, the mines had begun to take their toll on the Nazi war machine. Shipments of iron ore needed to manufacture armor-plated Panzer III and IV tanks had come to a near halt at a moment the Germans could ill-afford to stop production. At the same time, the German military was growing increasingly concerned that the Allies were preparing to stage an invasion through Norway.

One of the Nazis' menacing bulwarks against the Allies was a battleship so large it was classified as a "fleet in being," or a fleet all on its own. The ship, named the *Tirpitz*, had been built to destroy Royal Navy battleships. But its size also posed drawbacks. After a battle, the German navy sometimes needed three months to resupply the *Tirpitz* with fuel, so the vessel saw little fleet action. Instead, it typically spent its days in or near port guarding the Norwegian coastline.

For the Allies, the *Tirpitz* posed an alluring target, and they had unsuccessfully attempted to sink the ship after it was first launched. Finally, in November 1944, a squadron of Royal Air Force bombers located the *Tirpitz* in a Norwegian port. Over 800 feet long, the ship provided an excellent target. The bombers sent in two 12,000-pound bombs and blew a gigantic hole in the hull. The boat turned on its side, trapping and killing close to 1,000 men inside. The destruction of the *Tirpitz* was another blow to the Germans at a point in the war where they were losing ground.

Radar and U-Boats

German U-boats were stealthy and deadly, and they played a continuing role in the Battle of the Atlantic. U-boats had one weakness: They had to spend time on the surface each night to recharge their batteries and take on fresh air. The Allies' improved radar systems allowed their ships and aircraft to spot U-boats on the surface; many routine German patrols became suicide missions. To counter Allied attacks, some commanders coated their U-boats with tiles reducing their radar signature; this worked until the Allies upgraded their radar system, rendering the tiles less useful.

War & Technology— U-Boats and Sonar

The war at sea, on both sides, was often a battle of improving technology and tactics to counter new, ever-evolving technology. When the Allies started using convoys to counter the U-boat threat, the U-boats adjusted tactics to deal with escort ships. By the end of 1943, the Allies had begun to turn the tide of the war, thanks in large part to a detection technology that came to be known as sonar (Sound Navigation And Ranging).

1944

The Allies March North Through Italy

THE ATTACK CONTINUED ON WHAT BRITISH PRIME MINISTER
WINSTON CHURCHILL CALLED "THE SOFT UNDERBELLY OF EUROPE."

By the end of 1943, the Allies were well established in southern Italy and moving north. The German commander in charge of Italy, Albert Kesselring, hoped that rough terrain, poor weather, and the defensive lines, especially the fortified Winter Line south of Rome, would stop or at least delay the enemies' advance.

The Allies were stuck but thought they saw a way out. Suspecting that the Germans were using a mountaintop monastery near the Winter Line as a lookout, on February 15, troops dropped 1,400 tons of bombs on the historic Monte Cassino abbey, reducing it to rubble. Over the next five months, the Allies would assault the German-fortified position on Monte Cassino another four

times. The last attack, involving a strike to the west of the town in coordination with a new offensive to the north, finally forced the Germans to pull back on May 18.

A week later, the Germans had again retreated, eventually taking a new defensive position called the Gothic Line about 200 miles north of Rome, along the summits of the Apennine Mountains. It took the Allies three months to reach this location, but many of the troops who had been fighting in Italy began to be diverted for an assault on German positions in France. With their ranks depleted, the Allies were unable to break through the Gothic Line. The Italian effort stalled, and the Allies failed to make major advances before winter set in.

British, U.S., Canadian, French, and Polish forces joined in the fight at Monte Cassino.

Monte Cassino abbey after the attack. Using old plans, the abbey was rebuilt in the late 1940s.

"With very heavy hearts we are going to have to turn our weapons on the abbey."

—Allied leaflet dropped over Monte Cassino

Monte Cassino was founded in 526 by St. Benedict and was home to a vast library and valuable art collection. The manuscripts had been removed before the bombing, but a number of valuable pieces of art were destroyed during the attack. Many questioned whether it was truly necessary to bomb such a historic site.

The Bombing of the Abbey at Monte Cassino

It was British General Harold Alexander who authorized the controversial decision to bomb the abbey at Monte Cassino. Alexander was impressed with the tenacity of the German troops and wrote to Churchill that "the destruction caused in Cassino to roads and movement by bombing was so terrific that the employment of tanks or any other fighting vehicles has been seriously hampered. The tenacity of these German paratroops is quite remarkable, considering they were subjected to the whole Mediterranean Air Force plus the better part of 800 guns under greatest concentration of firepower which has ever been put down and lasting for six hours. I doubt if there are any other troops in the world who could have stood up to it and then gone on fighting with the ferocity they have..."

The Atlantic Wall, made of concrete barriers and bunkers, was augmented with heavy artillery. These defenses presented a formidable barrier to Allied forces.

1944

D-Day: The Invasion of Normandy

OPERATION OVERLORD, A BOLD PLAN TO OPEN THE WESTERN FRONT WAS FINALLY REALIZED, BUT ALLIED TROOPS WOULD PAY THE PRICE.

In early summer 1944, the German High Command knew that a huge Allied invasion was imminent. They mistakenly thought D-Day would take place near Calais, France, and this strategic error would lead to a turning point in the war.

The Germans had spent years constructing the Atlantic Wall, a series of defensive fortifications along the French coast near Calais: reinforced concrete guard posts for artillery positions and machine gunners, the laying of almost six million mines, and the placement of thousands of tank traps along the beaches.

Instead of coming ashore at Calais, British and American troops planned the largest amphibious attack in history on the five beaches well to the west, in Normandy. Weather would play a crucial role. The Allies had scheduled D-Day for June 5, but in order to ensure successful air support and troop landings, they needed clear skies and calm seas. Because predictions for the 5th called for storms, Allied generals gave the go-ahead for a June 6 invasion.

Just prior to the invasion, Allied air transporters dropped paratroopers behind German lines. Their mission was to disrupt the Germans' ability to move supplies to the front and to prevent the flow of critical information among the Nazi troops. The paratroopers blew up bridges to stall enemy reinforcements, who would be rushing to the coast.

Landing ships ferried troops, and they also transported ambulances. The one shown here was on its way to Omaha Beach.

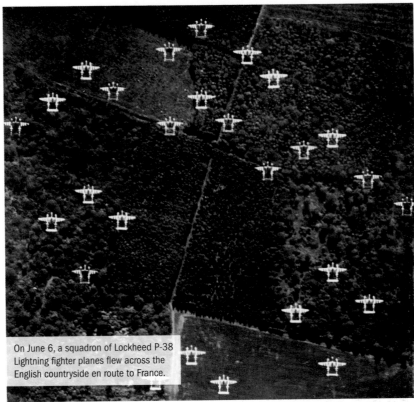

On June 6, a squadron of Lockheed P-38 Lightning fighter planes flew across the English countryside en route to France.

After coming ashore at Normandy, Allied troops prepared for their next move.

D-DAY BY THE NUMBERS

156,000
Allied troops

10,000
German troops

11,590
Aircraft

23,400
Airborne troops

127
Allied aircraft lost

12,000
Allied casualties

4,000–9,000
German casualties

Troops and tanks alike were loaded onto landing craft as the Allies prepared to cross the English Channel.

Soldiers of the Third Canadian Infantry Division set up antiaircraft guns on Juno Beach.

Diversion!

Prior to the Normandy invasion, the Allies made considerable effort to convince Germany that they were going to attack either in Norway or in Pas-de-Calais, France. Pre-invasion bombing was centered on Pas-de-Calais, and a huge camp of dummy tanks, tents, and landing craft was staged directly across the English Channel in southeastern Britain, where they would be seen and photographed by the Luftwaffe. The night before the invasion, dummy paratroopers were released to reinforce the belief that the assault would take place in Pas-de-Calais.

Operation Neptune, the naval portion of the D-Day invasion, consisted of almost 7,000 vessels of all sizes and kinds, including tugboats and minesweepers, from eight different navies. Warships were to provide cover for the transport vessels as they crossed the channel. Once the transport craft arrived at the French coast, warships bombarded German defenses. This heavy blitz damaged defensive fortifications, and when the guns were aimed further inland, the Germans were prevented from sending in reinforcements.

Sword Beach

On June 6, around 6:30 a.m., the Allies began their invasion of Normandy. Close to 7:30 a.m., British troops came ashore at Sword Beach, the easternmost beach of the invasion. They met minimal German resistance, and within 30 minutes of the landing, more than 28,000 British soldiers began moving inland. By 1 p.m., ground troops met with the airborne troops; their primary mission had been quickly accomplished.

Juno Beach

The Canadians landed on Juno Beach, just west of Sword Beach. Canadian troops faced far more resistance, including withering fire from two major artillery batteries, machine gunners hidden in pillbox guard posts, a high concrete sea wall, minefields, and a variety of beach obstacles. Heavy seas delayed the first wave of landing craft, allowing the Germans time to prepare. The first troops who came ashore suffered roughly 50 percent casualties. Nevertheless, the Canadians advanced further inland on D-Day than any other division. Even as the casualty rate slowed, losses mounted. Of the 21,400 Canadian troops who landed on Juno Beach, 1,200 did not survive the day.

Gold Beach

The British 50th Infantry Division came ashore at Gold Beach, west of the Canadians at Juno. The German battle plan called for the 352nd Division to defend Gold Beach, but troops had been ordered to leave their positions and pursue the

Approaching the French coast, a boat of Allied soldiers prepared to disembark.

Allied paratroopers who had come in the night before. By the time German troops returned to Gold Beach, the opportunity to counterattack had passed. The British were firmly in control of the beach. High sea levels had allowed them to pass over many of the mines and fortifications; they had also been able to land their tanks directly on the beach. By midnight, the British had landed 25,000 men, suffered only 400 casualties, moved six miles inland, and met up with the Canadians.

Omaha Beach

The American 1st and 29th Infantry Divisions attacked Omaha Beach, the next beach to the west. Of the beaches assaulted on D-Day, Omaha had the strongest defensive fortifications, including mortars, machine guns, and artillery. The beach also ended in steep cliffs, perfect spots for both artillery and snipers. Compounding these challenges were heavy seas and underwater obstacles. As a result, the majority of the landings had to take place away from planned locations.

American troops had to cross nearly 200 yards of open beach until they reached the protection of the seawall, and the first waves of troops suffered heavy casualties. By midday, only a few footholds had been secured. By the end of the day, the Americans, bolstered by small ad hoc infantry units, had secured the beachhead.

Utah Beach

The final major assault was on Utah Beach, the westernmost beach of the D-Day landings. U.S. airborne divisions had landed early in the morning, just inland from the beach. Many of the paratroopers lost their lives from drowning and enemy fire. When the U.S. 4th Infantry Division came ashore here, they joined the paratroopers and met little resistance. At the end of the day, 23,000 men had landed, with only 197 casualties.

The D-Day invasion was key to making the Western Front a viable threat to the German war machine. In August, Allied forces would liberate Paris, and then they would be on the march to Berlin.

The French Resistance and D-Day

Through coded messages in French-language BBC broadcasts, the French Resistance carried out specifically timed operations to sabotage railway lines, thus stalling German resupply routes. Resistance fighters cut railway lines in over 500 locations, effectively shutting down the railroads. The Resistance also destroyed electrical facilities, cutting off German communications.

D-Day: The First 24 Hours

General Dwight Eisenhower gave final instructions to paratroopers of the 101st Division.

Commanders of the British 6th Airborne Division synchronized their watches just before taking off for France.

0000–0100 HOURS

An assault unit boarded their landing craft, headed for Omaha Beach.

0400–0500 HOURS

The first landing craft and troops came ashore at Utah Beach.

0600–0700 HOURS

Canadian troops landed at Courseulles-sur-Mer, in the middle of Juno Beach, ready for battle.

0800–1000 HOURS

U.S. soldiers kept a wary eye out for enemy fire as they headed toward Omaha Beach.

1000–1200 HOURS

American paratroopers prepared to jump.
0100–0200 HOURS

The USS *Arkansas* shelled the beaches of Normandy, battering fortifications.
0400–0500 HOURS

Canadian infantry troops marched onto Juno Beach.
0700–0800 HOURS

American tanks and troops lined the shore at Omaha Beach.
0800–0900 HOURS

American reinforcements made their way onto Utah Beach.
1000–1200 HOURS

A barrage balloon sat atop Widerstandsnest 72, a concrete cave that was part of the Atlantic Wall.
1300–1400 HOURS

1944

Operation Bagration: The Soviet Army Pushes Back

IT WAS THE BEGINNING OF THE END FOR
THE NAZI TROOPS IN RUSSIA.

The largest Allied operation of World War II may also be the least known, primarily because it occurred on the Eastern Front, between the Soviet army and Nazi Germany's battle-weary Wehrmacht forces.

Operation Bagration, launched in the Soviet republic, Belorussia, and eastern Poland, on June 1944, coincided with the D-Day invasion of France. It was designed to force Germany to wage war on two fronts, east and west, to annihilate three German armies, and to decimate the German Army Group Centre. Geographically, this operation dwarfed the Normandy campaigns, and in just four weeks, the Germans lost more men than they had lost in five months of fighting at Stalingrad.

The main thrust of Operation Bagration was in Belorussia, where the Germans had several army groups consisting of nearly 40 divisions. The Russians had several advantages. They were fighting on home soil and knew the terrain. In addition, partisans helped out, and there were somewhere between 145,000 and 375,000 of them in Belorussia. Finally, German units were augmented by soldiers from conquered countries and by ethnic Germans who had been living in occupied territories. These soldiers were not always willing to lay down their lives for Germany.

Soviets fighting on the two northern fronts were directed by Marshal Aleksandr Vasilevsky, while Marshal Georgy Zhukov directed the two southern fronts. Each of the Soviet sectors involved in the offensive opened with a massive artillery barrage.

The well-armed Russians overwhelmed exhausted Germans who were still on Soviet soil in 1944.

Soviet troops faced no opposition as they patrolled the streets in Minsk, Belorussia, in 1944.

Thousands of German soldiers were taken prisoner in Belorussia. They were marched through the streets of Moscow in July 1944, but many would never make it to POW camps.

Soviet troops had to slog across rivers as they moved west toward Riga, 500 miles from Moscow.

Hundreds of thousands of soldiers followed the shelling, and they were supported by hundreds of T-34 tanks. German units were quickly overrun, and even though many willingly surrendered, the Red Army soldiers had little interest in taking prisoners. By August, the Germans had been pushed out of both Belorussia and eastern Poland.

Operation Bagration would be considered the worst of Hitler's many tactical blunders, primarily because he refused time and again to allow his field commanders to retreat and then regroup. All told, the German army lost more than 350,000 men in the offensive. Ten generals were killed, and another 21 were taken prisoner.

For the Soviets, Operation Bagration was a major victory. German troops would never again be on Russian soil, and Germany would never recover from the losses it sustained in Belorussia.

Furthermore, the former Soviet republics from the Crimea to the Baltic Sea were back in the Communist sphere.

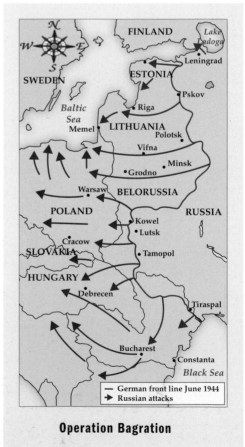

Operation Bagration

Soviet soldiers were on the move, defending their homeland.

Faces of War: Georgy Zhukov (1896–1974)

Soviet General Georgy Zhukov played a major role in Operation Bagration and in the Soviet drive to Berlin. As coordinator of the troop movements along the Eastern Front, he masterminded strategies that helped destroy 30 German army divisions during the assault and is credited with pushing the Germans completely out of Soviet territory. Zhukov became one of the most decorated officers in the history of the Soviet Union and Russia, and his skills were recognized by Allied leaders. He was also a participant at the Potsdam Conference.

American troops had no choice but to retreat in defeat after Operation Market Garden. Here, they marched through the ruins of Nijmegen.

> "There were many reasons why we did not gain complete success at Arnhem."
>
> —Field Marshal Bernard Montgomery

Dutch citizens tended to wounded soldiers and children as they waited for further medical attention.

Over 20,000 troops parachuted into the Netherlands for Market Garden.

Allied tanks captured and then crossed the bridge at Nijmegen during the ill-fated campaign.

1944

A Bridge Too Far: Operation Market Garden

THE ALLIES TOOK A RISK AND COMMITTED
A MAJOR BLUNDER IN THE NETHERLANDS.

To carve a pathway into Germany through the Netherlands, and to foil German plans to seize the corridor, the British launched a bold but risky scheme: Operation Market Garden. It started with the U.S. 101st and 82nd Airborne trying to secure vital bridges that spanned the rivers and canals on the border between the Netherlands and Germany. German attacks were so fierce that soldiers began to refer to the stretch of road north of Eindhoven as "Hell's Highway," and at the end of the first day, Allied troops had advanced just seven miles. Fighting between the defending German troops and the Allies was especially intense at the Dutch towns of Veghel, Grave, and Nijmegen. Each of these towns had a key bridge that the Allies were determined to take, and Veghel had two.

British Lieutenant-Colonel John Frost and about 740 men attacked and held the main road bridge at Arnhem. When they reached a German pillbox, a concrete building on the bridge that housed machine guns and antitank weapons, their gunfire ignited the ammunition stored there. Frost said that there was a series of explosions that lit the sky and that the noise sounded like machine-gun fire.

When one of the British soldiers saw armored cars coming across the bridge from the south, he thought they were British reinforcements. Instead, they were German troops who opened fire with antitank weapons. The British disabled several armored vehicles, but they could do nothing to stop the onslaught.

Frost and his troops held on to the Arnhem bridge through three days and four nights of bitter fighting. But without reinforcements to keep up the battle, the British soldiers were overwhelmed. Wounded from a mortar explosion, Frost surrendered from his burning headquarters building, which almost collapsed on him and 300 of his wounded men.

On the night of September 25, some of the British airborne troops were able to retreat south across the lower Rhine to safety. However, of the 10,000 British and Polish troops who landed around Arnhem, all but about 2,100 were killed or captured by the Germans. Operation Market Garden, the largest airborne operation of the war, ended in failure.

General Douglas MacArthur waded ashore in the Philippines with some of his men on October 20, 1944.

1944

Japan's Fortunes Fade: Battle of Leyte Gulf

THE EMPIRE MADE ONE FINAL STAND IN THE PACIFIC.

By October, the U.S. was determined to cut off Japan's access to raw materials in the Pacific and establish another stronghold for the Allies' final assault on the Japanese home islands. While General Douglas MacArthur wanted to achieve the goal by striking the Philippines—fulfilling a pledge he had made two years earlier to return to the territory—U.S. naval commanders wanted to bypass those islands and attack Taiwan instead.

The debate was finally settled when U.S. naval aircraft, which had continued bombing Japanese airfields, discovered several unguarded Japanese airstrips in the central Philippines. Returning pilots reported that they had destroyed 478 aircraft on the ground and had sunk 59 ships. After hearing those reports, Admiral William "Bull" Halsey, the Third Fleet commander, decided to attack.

What the U.S. naval commanders did not know at that time was that Japanese forces throughout the Philippines had been ordered not to oppose the Allied bombing raids, or even to show their strength, until they were ready for one final grand showdown, dubbed Plan Sho, or Victory. The Japanese

Leyte Island sh
Smoke from nav

Geysers erupted in the water around a Japanese heavy cruiser in Manila Bay after it was attacked. The cruiser sank soon after this photo was taken.

The bombing from American planes was intense, creating fires all along the Leyte shoreline.

bardment 10-20-44

Faces of War: Hiroo Onoda and the War That Never Ended

Lieutenant Hiroo Onoda, an intelligence officer for the Imperial Japanese Army, was sent to Lubang Island in December 1944 to destroy the port and the airstrip on the small island. He was given one other order: "Never surrender."

When Allied soldiers arrived on the island in February 1945, Onoda and three other soldiers escaped into the jungle.

Seven months later, on September 2, 1945, Japan capitulated and World War II was officially over. But Onoda, hiding in the jungle, didn't hear the news. While the rest of the world, including the civilians on Lubang, celebrated the end of the world's bloodiest war, Onoda continued to obey orders—for 30 more years.

Onoda finally emerged from the jungle in 1974, and when he did, he was feted in Japan as the ultimate Japanese warrior—the soldier who never surrendered.

High Command strategy was an all-or-nothing gambit. For Admiral Soemu Toyoda, in charge of Japan's Combined Fleet, anything short of a total victory would allow American planes to cut off his access to needed ammunition supplies from Japan and fuel from the East Indies.

To divide the huge American battalion, the Japanese navy split off a decoy fleet, moving ships to the north. Halsey took the bait, but scout planes uncovered the real Japanese strike force, and the Japanese decoy strategy unraveled.

The Battle of Leyte Gulf was short, starting on October 23 and ending on the 26th. In those few days, the Japanese lost 35 ships, including four carriers, the "invincible" *Musashi* and 21 other warships, and more than 10,000 airmen and sailors. The United States lost just five ships. With this irrecoverable loss, Japanese land forces in the Philippines could no longer plan on reinforcements, air cover, or gunnery support, nor could they retreat. They were left to fight to the death or surrender. Though Japan still had warships afloat, with the staggering defeat at Leyte Gulf, the Japanese navy ceased to play any role in the final months of the Pacific campaign.

In the end, the battle for Leyte was a lopsided victory. In fact, MacArthur called it "perhaps the greatest defeat in the military annals of the Japanese Army."

Firefighters aboard the USS *Intrepid* scrambled to extinguish fires after the ship was hit by a Japanese kamikaze pilot. It was the first time that the Japanese had used organized kamikaze strikes.

Crew members on the USS *Birmingham* tried to extinguish a fire on the USS *Princeton*, which had just been hit by a Japanese dive bomber.

Smoke screens were set to try to hide and protect U.S. warships in Leyte Gulf.

1944

The Battle of the Bulge: Hitler's Desperate Gamble

FOR THE GERMANS, A WELL-KEPT SECRET HELPED SECURE CRITICAL RESOURCES FOR DEMORALIZED TROOPS.

In the closing months of 1944, the German war machine was struggling. Fuel was running low, replacement parts were nonexistent, and German soldiers were surrendering en masse. With the holidays approaching, there was even talk among some American forces that they would be home by Christmas.

By early December, the Russians were winning battles all along the Eastern Front, and they were pursuing remnants of the German army across both Poland and Prussia. In the West, plans were made to end the stalemate at the Hürtgen Forest, east of the Belgian-German border, and then resume the sweep to Berlin.

What Allied intelligence had failed to learn was that the Germans had clandestinely positioned three armies inside the sprawling forest. Before dawn on December 16, thousands of Nazi field guns opened fire along a 60-mile front as 200,000 Wehrmacht soldiers advanced to the area. Hitler's Operation Autumn Mist—his last desperate move to seize the offensive—had begun.

Allied commanders were caught unprepared and their 80,000 soldiers, many facing battle for the first time, did not have winter gear or enough ammunition to counter this fierce attack. In the initial barrage, American units scrambled to the rear, hoping to avoid the artillery onslaught. Nazi tanks and mechanized infantry seized huge chunks of land and captured stragglers. The Germans had driven a wedge 70 miles wide and 50 miles deep and split American and British troops, and hence the name, Battle of the Bulge.

Fighting in the Ardennes
The Allies had seriously miscalculated German offensive plans and had not prepared for a major attack in the heavy Belgian forests.

U.S. soldiers marched out of Bastogne, Belgium, just after ending the siege of the town.

German infantrymen hurried past burning American trucks captured during the Battle of the Bulge.

American soldiers patrolled the town of St. Vith, just east of Vielsalm, in January 1945.

American soldiers watched for attacking German military forces as they slowly advanced through the forest.

Fighting at Bastogne

The Germans had the Allies on the run, and there was indeed a race to get to the town of Bastogne. Faulty German intelligence reports indicated that thousands of Allied troops were waiting there to counterattack. The Americans actually had few defenses in the town, but they were sending in reinforcements. For nearly a week, the Americans at Bastogne held out, slowly giving ground, while sustaining heavy losses from enemy bombardment and harassing fire. Finally, Allied units broke through the German lines and were able to relieve the beleaguered defenders.

Many German units, most notably the Panzer tanks, were running out of fuel. For the American units opposing them, it was just a matter of zeroing in and decimating them with field artillery and tank fire. Eight hundred tanks were destroyed. The remaining German Panzer crews had two options: They could die inside their tanks or surrender. Thousands chose to surrender.

The battles continued through the holidays, but finally on December 28, Hitler conceded defeat. For the Allies, the road to Berlin suddenly became clear.

British Prime Minister Winston Churchill would call the Battle of the Bulge "undoubtedly the greatest American battle of the war," though the troops paid a heavy toll for the victory.

U.S. soldiers took their positions and fired at enemy-held positions just after Christmas. The army forces emerged victorious from the battle.

Brigadier General Anthony McAuliffe

On December 22, General McAuliffe (1898–1975) was asked to surrender at Bastogne. Even though his troops were completely surrounded by German forces, his now-famous response was "Nuts!"

McAuliffe graduated from West Point in 1918 and parachuted into Normandy on D-Day. After the Battle of the Bulge, he was given command of the 103rd Infantry Division, which he led until the end of the war.

BATTLE OF THE BULGE BY THE NUMBERS

Allies

American casualties

82,000

19,000
killed

40,000
wounded

23,000
captured or missing

800
tanks

British casualties

1,408

200
killed

969
wounded

239
missing

German casualties

84,834

60,000–100,000
killed, missing, captured,
or wounded

600
tanks and assault guns
Hundreds of aircraft

Estimated numbers

Paratrooper Equipment

1. Reserve Parachute Made of white silk, it came with a cover.

2. Helmet The steel helmets were green and had a rough textured finish.

3. Jacket and Pants Cargo pants were issued only to paratroopers. German propaganda labeled paratroopers "the butchers with the big pockets."

4. Jump Boots Designed for jumping and landing, they helped prevent injuries.

5. M1A1 Thompson With a 20-round magazine and .45 caliber ammunition, the Thompson was an effective close-combat weapon.

6. First Aid Pouch It contained bandages and sulfamite powder, used to prevent infection.

7. Fighting Knife The M3 trench knife was introduced in 1943.

8. Web Belt It held ammunition, a shovel, and canteen. The shovel folded, had a pointed end, and could be used as a pick.

9. Pistol Shown here, with extra ammunition, is a .45 caliber pistol that could fire eight shots.

10. Evasion Kit It included a map, a compass, and a tiny hacksaw. One type of compass was worn on the wrist.

11. Cricket Noisemaker One click was met by two clicks to identify friend from enemy.

12. Fragmentation Grenade The cast-iron hand grenade was about the size of a lemon. They were filled with TNT, had a "blast radius" of about 30 yards, and a kill radius of five to 10 yards.

Paratroopers carried between 70 and 120 pounds of equipment as they jumped into battle.

2

8

3

4

8 | THE END OF THE WAR

1945: BY EARLY 1945, IT WAS CLEAR THE CONFLICT WAS DRAWING TO A CLOSE, BUT PEACE WOULD COME AT AN ASTRONOMICAL PRICE AND WOULD SET THE STAGE FOR THE COLD WAR.

An Allied bomber made a daylight raid over Berlin, weakening the city before it was barraged with artillery fire by the Soviets in April 1945.

"Surrender is forbidden."

—Adolf Hitler

1945

Shaping a Postwar World

IN EARLY 1945, THREE KEY ALLIED LEADERS MET IN YALTA
AND DRAFTED AN AGREEMENT THAT WOULD CHANGE HISTORY.

In February 1945, President Franklin D. Roosevelt made the arduous journey to Yalta on the Crimean Peninsula to meet with Prime Minister Winston Churchill and Premier Joseph Stalin. With the war in its final stages, the three Allied leaders gathered to discuss the impending surrender of Germany and Japan and to decide what a postwar world would look like. Their first order of business was to demand unconditional surrender from Germany and Japan.

The leaders came to Yalta with different agendas. Churchill hoped to maintain the British Empire, while Stalin wanted to expand the USSR and strengthen its power. Although fighting was going fairly well in the Pacific, Roosevelt and Churchill knew more had to be done to defeat the Japanese. They wanted Stalin to agree to enter the war in the Pacific once the conflict in Europe was over. To win Stalin's support, Roosevelt secretly agreed that once the Japanese were defeated, he would reinstate privileges the Soviets had lost in Manchuria, such as control of a key port and of the railroad. Churchill was never informed of the negotiations.

Stalin and Roosevelt held a number of discussions at the Yalta Conference. Despite their differing postwar agendas, the two leaders came together to end the war and rid Germany of the Nazi regime.

Allied leaders convened at the Yalta Conference from February 4 to 11, 1945. Seated left to right: Prime Minister Winston Churchill, President Franklin D. Roosevelt, and Premier Joseph Stalin. Two months later, on April 12, Roosevelt passed away.

1945: A Year of Victory

Events on different fronts brought World War II to a close as the Allied nations reached final victory.

1945 JAN

JANUARY 12 The Soviets liberated Warsaw.

MARCH 7 U.S. troops crossed the Rhine River at Remagen.

MARCH

APRIL 16 The Soviets launched their final offensive, encircling Berlin.

APRIL

APRIL 30 Hitler committed suicide at his bunker in Berlin.

MAY 7 Germany surrendered to the Western Allies.

MAY 9 Germany surrendered to the Soviets.

MAY

AUGUST 6 The U.S. dropped an atomic bomb on Hiroshima.

AUGUST 8 The Soviet Union declared war on Japan and invaded Manchuria.

AUGUST

SEPT

AUGUST 9 The United States dropped an atomic bomb on Nagasaki.

SEPTEMBER 2 Japan formally surrendered, ending World War II.

World leaders and their advisors worked together for a week at the Yalta Conference. General George C. Marshall, who would later author the Marshall Plan, and Admiral William D. Leahy were seated to the right with Roosevelt.

1945

A Punishment to Fit the Crime

AT YALTA, ALLIED LEADERS DECIDED TO SPLIT GERMANY AND REQUIRE THE COUNTRY TO PAY REPARATIONS.

During the Yalta conference, Allied leaders also discussed the future of postwar Germany and eastern Europe. Churchill, Roosevelt, and Stalin agreed to divide Germany into four zones of occupation. They decided that France, Britain, the U.S., and the Soviet Union would each take responsibility for one region and that Germany would have to demilitarize and throw off all vestiges of Nazism.

The three leaders also stipulated that all future governments in eastern Europe would be "friendly" to the Soviet government. In exchange, Stalin would allow free elections in all the liberated countries in the Soviet sphere of influence. The leader of the USSR won an additional concession from his conference partners—that Communists would have a role in Poland's future national government.

In the United States, the Yalta Accord was initially celebrated as a breakthrough that would ensure the peace. The agreement seemed to guarantee continued cooperation between the Americans and Soviets into the postwar world. By the spring of 1945, however, those hopes were dashed, as the USSR and the United States put themselves on a collision course for another, more ideologically driven conflict—the Cold War.

Churchill (left) shook hands with Stalin (right) outside the Livadia Palace in Yalta. The friendly relations displayed for the camera belied a tension that existed between the leaders, who had incompatible postwar goals.

When Roosevelt addressed Congress about plans made at the Yalta Conference, a national audience tuned in.

In February, U.S. marines were pinned on the beach of Iwo Jima, bombarded by Japanese artillery.

1945
The Shores of Iwo Jima

IN THE FIRST AMERICAN ATTACK ON JAPANESE SOIL, U.S. MARINES FOUGHT TENACIOUSLY.

Island Hopping

U.S. forces in the Pacific followed a strategy of moving from island to island, known as island hopping. They captured some islands held by the Japanese, skipped others, and continued on a steady path to Japan. From Tarawa and Makin in the Gilbert Islands, troops moved to Eniwetok and Kwajalein in the Marshall Islands. Then, they pushed on to Saipan, Tinian, and Guam in the Marianas.

Located some 660 miles south of Tokyo in the Pacific Ocean, Iwo Jima was a strategic Japanese-held island that, if captured, could serve as a base for American fighter planes and bombers.

In February 1945, the Americans decided to take Iwo Jima. Beginning on the 19th, the U.S. Navy heavily bombed the island, paving the way for two marine divisions to storm onto its beaches.

The attack did little to hurt enemy forces, who were strategically entrenched in Iwo Jima's many caves. During the 36 days of fighting, nearly 7,000 marines were killed and another 20,000 were wounded. The toll for the Japanese was even higher. Of the island's 18,000 defenders, only 216 were captured; the rest perished.

Once the marines had secured Iwo Jima, the island served as a landing base for more than 2,200 B-29 bombers that would fly against the Japanese homeland.

Mount Suribachi

Perhaps the most iconic image of World War II is a controversial photo taken on Iwo Jima five days after fighting on the island began. Although some have suggested the image was staged, it was not. Instead, on the morning of February 23, a group of marines fought their way to the top of a strategic peak, Mount Suribachi, and planted a small flag. Later in the day, five marines and a naval corpsman returned with a second, larger flag, and Associated Press photographer Joe Rosenthal was on hand to capture the moment. The photo was quickly wired across the globe and reproduced in many U.S. newspapers.

U.S. marines successfully blew up a cave connected to a Japanese blockhouse on Iwo Jima.

Fighting at Iwo Jima lasted more than a month, but five days into the struggle, U.S. servicemen triumphantly raised the American flag on Mount Suribachi. Of the men pictured here, only three survived the battle.

On February 19, Operation Detachment, the U.S. marine invasion of Iwo Jima, began. At the end of the day, more than 550 marines had lost their lives and another 1,800 had been wounded.

Factories were a prime target during the bombings of Tokyo, but eventually most of the city was leveled.

B-29 Superfortress

The B-29 Superfortress was indeed a flying citadel. The plane had a pressurized cabin and was designed for long distance and high altitude. Each of its four engines had two turbosuperchargers, which permitted the plane to cruise at elevations over 40,000 feet. Turrets, which were remotely controlled from inside the pressurized cabin, housed machine guns, and the tail turret carried a cannon. This long-range plane flew mostly in the Pacific, where it could speed along at over 350 miles per hour. The *Enola Gay*, a Superfortress, was modified in order to carry the atomic bomb. It had new propellers, stronger engines, and its bomb bay doors opened faster than those of most B-29s.

1945

Tokyo in Flames

EVEN BEFORE THE ATOMIC BOMB WAS DROPPED, U.S. WARPLANES HAD DEVASTATED JAPAN.

Having recently captured the Mariana Islands, about 1,500 miles from Japan in the South Pacific, the U.S. was finally in a position to strike the Japanese capital. On March 9, U.S. warplanes took off from airstrips on the volcanic isles of Tinian and Saipan and dropped more than 2,000 tons of incendiary bombs on Tokyo.

The weapons fell in clusters in the downtown area as well as the suburb of Shitamachi, where nearly three-quarters of a million people lived and worked, mostly in wooden-framed buildings.

More than 330 bombers, flying at only 500 feet, dropped their loads, creating a massive firestorm that was fanned by 30-knot winds. Terrified civilians tried to escape the conflagration, but crews aboard the bombers could smell burning flesh below.

Bombing raids in the spring and summer of 1945 leveled entire city blocks of downtown Tokyo, leaving people homeless and destitute.

Kamikaze pilots bowed to their leaders before taking off on their final, sacrificial flight, in which they turned their planes into deadly missiles.

1945

Suicide Pilots

TRAINED TO TAKE OFF, BUT NOT TO LAND, KAMIKAZE PILOTS BECAME AN INSTRUMENT OF TERROR.

Faces of War

"I firmly believe that the only way to swing the war in our favor is to resort to crash-dive attacks with our planes," said Japanese naval Captain Motoharu Okamura. "There will be more than enough volunteers for this chance to save our country."

When Mongolian emperor Kublai Khan unleashed warships to attack Japan in 1281, the small island nation was saved by terrifying ocean storms, referred to as the Divine Wind or kamikaze, which smashed the invading fleet.

Over 650 years later, with the Americans moving closer to their homeland, the Japanese hoped another Divine Wind would save their country. In 1945, however, the kamikazes would be suicidal pilots who would fly their airplanes into American warships.

Kamikaze pilots needed little training and were often university students motivated by family and national loyalty.

To them, defeat and surrender meant disgrace. Before taking off in planes laden with massive bomb loads, the pilots would hold religious ceremonies and pray. About 4,000 Japanese pilots sacrificed their lives this way, with almost 15 percent of them hitting their target.

One of the most successful use of kamikazes by the Japanese was the battle for Okinawa, where 300 aircraft were flown into the American fleet. The destroyer *Laffey* was hit by 20 planes at once, but it did not sink, earning it the name "The Ship that Would Not Die." By the war's end, the kamikazes had sunk or damaged some 300 U.S. ships, killing or injuring 15,000 people.

U.S. forces had to mount harsh tactics against determined kamikaze pilots. Here, the USS *Missouri* was under attack off the coast of Okinawa.

Fewer than 15 percent of kamikaze missions met their targets. When they did, however, they devastated ships and crew.

On May 11, the USS *Bunker Hill* was hit by Japanese kamikazes near Okinawa, resulting in 372 deaths and 264 wounded.

Soviet rocket launchers could fire several rockets at once, a deadly tool in the Battle of Berlin. The haunting moans of the rockets earned them the name "Stalin's Organ" and made them an effective tool in psychological warfare.

Inside Hitler's Bunker

In January 1945, Hitler had moved into the bombproof *Fuhrerbunker* underneath the Reich Chancellery in Berlin, and from April 20 on, Hitler and his top aides remained safe in the hideout. On April 29, Hitler and his longtime companion, Eva Braun, were married there. On April 30, with the Soviets only yards away, Hitler and Braun committed suicide.

1945

Racing to Exact Revenge

THE GERMANS' WORST FEARS WERE REALIZED WHEN THE SOVIETS BEAT THE ALLIES TO BERLIN.

The failure of Adolf Hitler's Ardennes offensive left the bulk of Germany's troops in the East trying to slow the Soviet advance. For American and British troops approaching Berlin, the path was wide open.

Gunning for the Reichstag

Stalin was determined to enter Berlin before the Allies. On March 9, he ordered Generals Georgy Zhukov and Ivan Konev to reach the city as quickly as possible. By April 16, the Russians had crossed the Oder River in Poland and began transporting thousands of troops across the river's 25 bridges.

The Soviets began to unleash a terrifying barrage of artillery fire west of the Oder against Nazi fortifications. When Zhukov's troops advanced, they found that the Germans had retreated to defensive positions further inland, but the Germans continued to fight. It took Zhukov three days to break the new German defensive line, but once he did, he sent in huge numbers of Soviet tanks and blanketed Berlin with rocket fire. German troops quickly mounted a strong defense. But on April 26, more than 500,000 Soviet troops attacked the center of Berlin, and fighting occurred building by building. Red Army soldiers made their way to the Reichstag, the parliament building and symbol of Nazi power. After killing government defenders, the Russian troops raised the Soviet flag, and on May 2, the guns stopped firing.

Hundreds of thousands of soldiers and civilians perished in the Battle of Berlin. But it was the death of Hitler that signaled the end of the Third Reich.

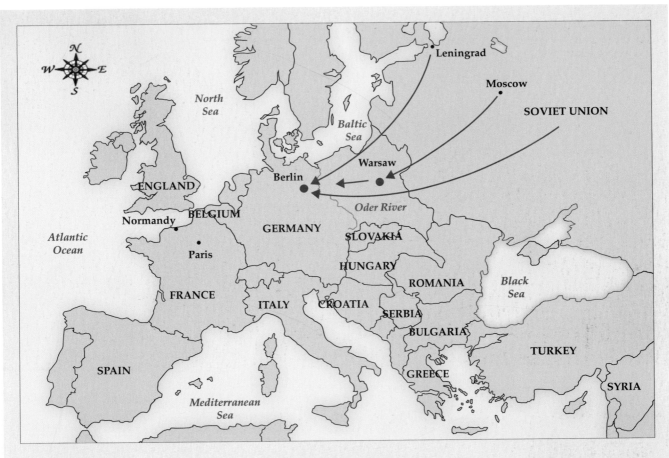

Soviet Routes West to Berlin

In 1945, Soviet T-34 tanks advanced on Berlin. Tanks like this one broke through German defenses and fired tons of shells into the beleaguered city.

On June 3, a German civilian stopped to examine a giant painting of Stalin in the conquered city of Berlin. One dictator had replaced another.

In just two months in 1944, over 430,000 Hungarian Jews were deported to Auschwitz.

1945

Liberation of the Concentration Camps

WHAT THE ALLIES DISCOVERED ON THEIR MARCH
THROUGH GERMANY HORRIFIED THE WORLD.

While there had been rumors and some public awareness of the persecution of Jews, Roma, and others that the Nazis deemed "undesirable," the world had no idea of the extent of the genocide Germany was inflicting on the civilian population in Nazi-occupied territories. Shipped to camps in crowded trains and forced into concentration camps, millions of Jews and others would perish in intolerable circumstances.

The extent of the horrors first became known when the Russians reached Majdanek, near Lublin, Poland, during the summer of 1944. Here, Germans had tried to hide evidence of mass murders by demolishing the camp. The Soviets also passed through the camp at Sobibor in eastern Poland, where more than 250,000 people had been killed. In early 1945, the Soviets liberated Auschwitz, located in southern Poland. It was the last extermination camp still in operation near the end of the war, and it was the largest. Here, Soviet soldiers discovered the gas chambers and large crematoria. More than one million prisoners died at Auschwitz, and 90 percent were Jewish.

Young men held prisoner at Dachau cheered the American troops who liberated the camp.

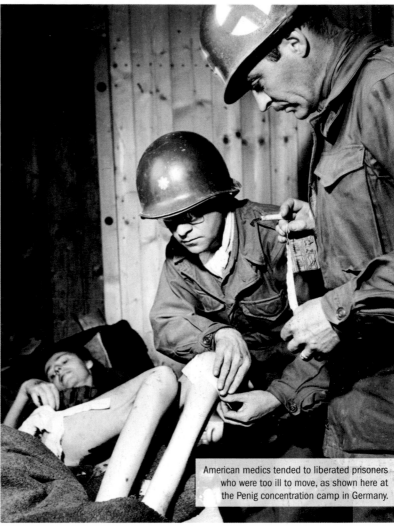

American medics tended to liberated prisoners who were too ill to move, as shown here at the Penig concentration camp in Germany.

In April 1945, Americans discovered other forced labor facilities, and on April 11, they liberated the camp at Buchenwald, freeing more than 20,000 prisoners. Americans also liberated Dachau and Mauthausen, which had its own gas chamber and where tens of thousands perished.

Later that month, the British liberated Bergen-Belsen, 45 miles south of Hamburg. Here, over 50,000 prisoners were found, suffering from starvation, dehydration, and lack of sanitation. Many were too weak to respond to their liberators. The British also discovered the unburied corpses of 20,000, who had died in appalling conditions.

Medical teams came to the camps to help save those they could, but thousands died despite the efforts of the Allied forces. For those prisoners who survived, recovery would be a long, painful road. The images of the camps and the survivors did much to inform the world of the atrocities. Many of those responsible for the genocide would stand trial at Nuremberg and faced death sentences for their actions.

The mood was somber on May 7 when German military commander Alfred Jodl signed the German Instrument of Surrender. Seated left to right are Major Wilhelm Oxenius, Jodl, and Admiral Hans-Georg von Friedburg.

1945

Total Capitulation

GERMAN GENERAL ALFRED JODL
SURRENDERED HIS PEOPLE TO A VICTOR
HE HOPED WOULD BE GENEROUS.

On May 7, General Alfred Jodl, representing the German High Command, signed the unconditional surrender of his forces in Europe. Jodl had come to General Dwight Eisenhower's headquarters in Reims, France, hoping to yield only to the Americans and British fighting in the western part of the continent, but Eisenhower demanded total capitulation of all German troops in the East as well. Jodl radioed Germany's new leader, Grand Admiral Karl Donitz, and asked for permission to sign the surrender documents. Donitz agreed.

V-E Day

The defeat of Germany was celebrated around the world. In London, New York, and thousands of other cities, jubilant crowds took to the streets in a massive outpouring. Men, women, and children danced, sang, and waved flags in the streets. People hugged, kissed, and proposed toasts. Soldiers slapped each other on the back; many simply said, "I survived."

On May 8, 1945, massive crowds gathered in Piccadilly Circus, London, to celebrate V-E Day. More than one million people in London alone came out to celebrate the victory.

On V-E Day, Churchill gave a radio broadcast to the world, announcing that the war with Germany had been won.

Children helped a British woman put up the Union Jack as they celebrated V-E Day.

1945

The Manhattan Project

ROOSEVELT HAD BEEN KEEN TO HAVE THE FIRST ATOMIC
WEAPON EVEN BEFORE WORLD WAR II BEGAN.

While victory in Europe had been won, the war in the Pacific was still raging. At home in the United States, scientists were working to develop new armaments through a highly classified program termed the Manhattan Project.

This new weapons research dated to October 1939, when President Roosevelt learned from a special advisory committee that uranium would provide more destructive power than any known explosive material. Roosevelt decided to pursue the use of uranium in bombs and named physicist and University of California Berkeley physics professor J. Robert Oppenheimer to lead the endeavor.

Oppenheimer was one of the few people at the time who understood the

-2-

The United States has only very poor ores of uranium in moderate quantities. There is some good ore in Canada and the former Czechoslovakia, while the most important source of uranium is Belgian Congo.

In view of this situation you may think it desirable to have some permanent contact maintained between the Administration and the group of physicists working on chain reactions in America. One possible way of achieving this might be for you to entrust with this task a person who has your confidence and who could perhaps serve in an inofficial capacity. His task might comprise the following:

a) to approach Government Departments, keep them informed of the further development, and put forward recommendations for Government action, giving particular attention to the problem of securing a supply of uranium ore for the United States;

b) to speed up the experimental work, which is at present being carried on within the limits of the budgets of University laboratories, by providing funds, if such funds be required, through his contacts with private persons who are willing to make contributions for this cause, and perhaps also by obtaining the co-operation of industrial laboratories which have the necessary equipment.

I understand that Germany has actually stopped the sale of uranium from the Czechoslovakian mines which she has taken over. That she should have taken such early action might perhaps be understood on the ground that the son of the German Under-Secretary of State, von Weizsäcker, is attached to the Kaiser-Wilhelm-Institut in Berlin where some of the American work on uranium is now being repeated.

Yours very truly,

A. Einstein

(Albert Einstein)

Albert Einstein's letter to President Roosevelt, written on August 2, 1939, revealed how heavily involved Roosevelt was in the making of the atomic bomb.

On July 16, Robert Oppenheimer, wearing a white hat, and General Leslie Groves, next to Oppenheimer, inspected the Trinity atomic bomb test site at the Alamogordo Bombing and Gunnery Range.

potential power of the atom, and his first task was to figure out how much uranium-235 would be needed to sustain a nuclear chain reaction. He summoned to Berkeley some of the brightest physicists in the world, including the German-born Hans Bethe and Hungarian Edward Teller.

Separately, a team of scientists led by Italian physicist Enrico Fermi scored a major breakthrough on December 2, 1942, when they demonstrated the world's first controlled nuclear reaction at the University of Chicago. The achievement was considered so important, the government poured additional funds into the Manhattan Project, building nuclear facilities at Oak Ridge, Tennessee, and Hanford, Washington. The atomic bomb itself would be put together at an assembly plant in Los Alamos, New Mexico.

Top Secret

Secrecy at Los Alamos was of the utmost importance, and of the 120,000 employees on site, only a small circle of scientists knew of the bomb's development. Even Vice President Harry S. Truman was kept in the dark, and Roosevelt and Churchill agreed not to inform Stalin. The world would later learn that Stalin knew about Los Alamos through a spy, a German Communist refugee and British scientist named Klaus Fuchs. Fuchs had fled Nazi Germany in 1933, continued his studies in Scotland, and in 1943, he was sent to the United States to work on the Manhattan Project.

Klaus Fuchs was part of the Manhattan Project's inner circle. Convicted of espionage in 1950, he served a nine-year prison sentence in Britain.

Dr. Enrico Fermi received the Nobel Prize in Physics in 1938 and soon thereafter emigrated to the United States.

An atomic explosion filled the sky over Alamogordo, New Mexico, on July 16.

1945

The Nuclear Age

THE SUCCESS OF THE TRINITY TEST USHERED IN THE
END OF THE WAR AND THE DAWNING OF A NEW ERA.

By the summer of 1945, scientists were ready to test the device that had taken six years to create. At 5:30 a.m. on July 16, in a remote section of the Alamogordo Air Base in New Mexico, the first full-scale test of an atomic fission bomb took place.

Destroyer of Worlds

The explosion was described as both magnificent and humbling. A bright mushroom cloud ascended over the desert sky, reaching a height of 40,000 feet. The blast was so great that it blew out windows of homes nearly 100 miles away.

Those who saw the test, code-named Trinity, said they would never forget it. Some observers laughed, others cried. Later, Oppenheimer recalled that a line from the "Bhagavad Gita" crossed his mind: "Now I am become Death—the destroyer of worlds."

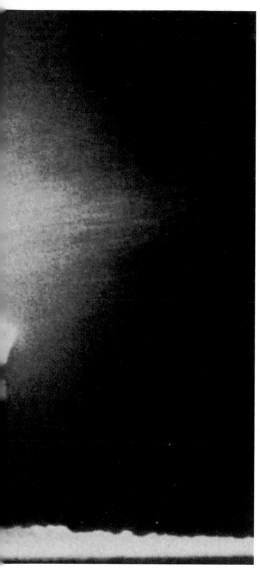

The tower used in the detonation of Gadget, the first bomb tested, was located in the middle of the Trinity nuclear site.

Faces of War

"For the first time in history there was a nuclear explosion. And what an explosion!," wrote General Leslie Groves, head of the Manhattan Project for the Army Corps of Engineers, to his superiors back in Washington. "The bomb was not dropped from an airplane but was exploded on a platform on top of a 100-foot high steel tower. The test was successful beyond the most optimistic expectations of anyone."

The atomic bomb, code-named Little Boy, rested on a trailer cradle in a bomb pit at Tinian Airbase, North Marianas Islands. The bomb was dropped on Hiroshima on August 6.

Fat Man and Little Boy

The next step in the Manhattan Project was to construct two bombs that could be dropped from an airplane. Scientists had given those weapons two nicknames: Fat Man and Little Boy.

Fat Man weighed 10,800 pounds and packed an explosive force of 21,000 tons of TNT.

As its name implied, Little Boy was slightly smaller, but it still had a huge explosive capability of about 15,000 tons.

The atomic bomb code-named Fat Man was lowered onto a trailer cradle at Tinian Airbase. It was dropped on Nagasaki on August 9.

1945

The Allies Invade Okinawa

THE LAST GREAT BATTLE OF WORLD WAR II WAS ALSO THE LARGEST SEA-LAND-AIR CONFRONTATION IN HISTORY.

Japan had made it clear it would not surrender. The Allies knew that to end the war in the Pacific, they would have to invade Japan, and to do so, they needed to take Okinawa, a large island located 350 miles south of the main island.

Okinawa would be the perfect place to launch an invasion of the main island. It would also serve as a strategic base to begin a massive aerial and naval bombing campaign that would weaken Japanese defenses.

The battle for Okinawa, known as "Operation Iceberg," began on April 1, 1945, as 60,000 U.S. marines and soldiers stormed ashore. The Japanese did not resist the landings; instead, they hunkered down in concrete guardhouses, caves, and ancient castles, which proved formidable defensive structures.

The Americans easily overpowered the Japanese defending the northern part of the island. But things were different in the south, where Japanese soldiers were prepared to fight until death. Heavy rain turned the battle into a muddy, bloody slog.

Fighting lasted for 82 long days. The U.S. reported about 50,000 troops killed, missing, or wounded, but in the end, took Okinawa.

Rockets from an American ship streamed toward Okinawa Island just before the invasion by the U.S. 10th Army forces.

A U.S. Navy Chance-Vought F4U Corsair fighter plane fired its load of rocket projectiles against a Japanese stronghold on Okinawa.

A U.S. marine armed with a submachine gun took fire at a Japanese sniper at Wana Ridge on South Okinawa.

American troops helped move residents of Okinawa away from the front lines.

1945

A Different Kind of War

WITH AN ATOMIC BOMB IN HIS ARSENAL, TRUMAN HAD
THE POWER TO MAKE DEMANDS AT POTSDAM.

On April 12, 1945, President Roosevelt, who had been in declining health, passed away and was succeeded by his vice president, Harry S Truman. It was not until this transition that Truman was briefed on the Manhattan Project. Three months later, he learned of the successful test of the world's first atomic bomb while attending the Potsdam Conference with Churchill and Stalin, helping to chart out postwar punishment for the Nazis.

Truman was soon to make one of the most fateful decisions in world history: to use the bomb against Japan. From Truman's perspective and that of other U.S. leaders, there was little choice. The Japanese were fighting ferociously on Okinawa and elsewhere, inflicting heavy casualties on Allied forces.

Invading the Japanese home island was the next logical step, but military planners told Truman that American casualties could total one million. Those who supported the bomb's use not only believed it would end the war quickly, but that it would make the U.S. the dominant force in reshaping the postwar world. Truman considered the gravity of the situation and, over the objections of some of his key advisors, ordered the use of the atomic bomb.

Churchill (left), President Harry S Truman (center), and Stalin (right) shared a moment of celebration and unity at Potsdam. A major issue for Truman was how to handle Germany. He did not want a repeat of the Treaty of Versailles.

In early August 1945, leaders from the United States, Britain, and the Soviet Union met in Potsdam to discuss Germany's punishment, the restoring of order, and balance of power in the postwar world.

The atomic bomb explosion over Hiroshima sent a giant mushroom cloud into the atmosphere. Colonel Paul Tibbets, the pilot, later described it as "boiling upward like something terribly alive."

Tibbets stood next to the *Enola Gay*, the B-29 he piloted over Hiroshima.

1945

Destination Hiroshima

LITTLE BOY DESTROYED 90 PERCENT
OF A JAPANESE CITY IN SECONDS.

On July 26, 1945, the United States, the United Kingdom, and China called for the unconditional surrender of Japan in the Potsdam Declaration. Should Japan refuse, "prompt and utter destruction" would ensue. Japan ignored the ultimatum. On August 6, 1945, the B-29 Superfortress *Enola Gay* left the island of Tinian carrying Little Boy. At the controls was Colonel Paul W. Tibbets, and the target on this day was Hiroshima. With a population of about 340,000,

Hiroshima was chosen because it had suffered little damage during the war, and the weather over the city was clear.

The crew armed the bomb as Tibbets climbed to 30,000 feet. At 8 a.m., Hiroshima came into view. Thirteen minutes later, 26-year-old Major Thomas Ferebee, the bombardier, made sure the target was in sight and prepared to drop the weapon. At 8:15 a.m., the bomb bay doors opened and Little Boy dropped away, earning a place in history.

Once the bomb had been released, Tibbets swung the plane away from the blast. A half-minute after detonation, the *Enola Gay*, 2,000 feet above the city, was rocked by tremendous shock waves. The mushroom cloud of destruction reached 40,000 feet into the atmosphere. Some 80,000 people, most of whom were Japanese civilians, were instantly vaporized. By the end of 1945, the casualty figures climbed to approximately 140,000. Many died from burns they sustained during the blast or from illnesses related to radiation.

One month after the atomic bomb was dropped on
Hiroshima, a war correspondent surveyed the destruction.

The effect of the bomb was felt more than one mile away from
its detonation point, and fires spread over four square miles.

Destination Nagasaki

Unfortunately, the destruction of Hiroshima did not convince the Japanese to surrender to the Allies. A second, more powerful atomic bomb was necessary to change their minds.

Three days after the dropping of Little Boy, Major Charles Sweeney, in another B-29, released Fat Man on Nagasaki, a secondary target. Some 75,000 people were killed immediately. It was the last major act of World War II.

In the years since the bombings of Hiroshima and Nagasaki, many have questioned the morality of the use of such devastating force to convince Japan to surrender. Many of those affected by the bombs were civilians who had no part in the war. Of those who survived the blasts, many suffered unimaginable wounds and horrific burns. Thousands of others would later be diagnosed with cancer and various health issues as a result of their exposure to radiation.

Critics have argued that the bombings were barbaric and were not necessary. However, for those responsible for the atomic bomb and its deployment, the ends justified the means. As President Truman explained in a speech, "It was my responsibility as president to force the Japanese war lords to come to terms as quickly as possible with the minimum loss of lives. I then made my final decision. And that final decision was mine alone to make . . ."

In this photo taken in September 1945, Lt. Colonel Kermit Beahan, who dropped the bomb over Nagasaki, waved from his plane.

A second atomic bomb was dropped on Japan on August 9. The attack led to Japan's unconditional surrender.

After the fires had been extinguished, a Japanese citizen surveyed the damaged lands around Nagasaki. The bombing was confined to the Urikami Valley where the Mitsubishi munition plant was located.

On August 15, Truman announced Japan's surrender at a White House press conference.

1945

Finally, The End

HIROHITO SAID HE SURRENDERED TO AVOID THE "TOTAL EXTINCTION OF HUMAN CIVILIZATION."

In the wake of the Soviet invasion of Manchuria on August 9 and the dropping of the atomic bombs on Hiroshima and Nagasaki, Emperor Hirohito on August 15 surrendered his country unconditionally. To alert his countrymen to the decision, Hirohito went on national radio for the first time ever and explained his reasoning. "We have resolved to pave the way for a grand peace for all the generations to come by enduring the unendurable and suffering what is insufferable," he said.

American forces soon occupied Japan under the command of Douglas MacArthur. Hirohito was not deposed, and he retained his position as emperor. He was, however, forced to renounce his divine status. Following Japan's surrender, it was determined that Emperor Hirohito would not be charged with any war crimes.

From the decks of the USS *Missouri* on September 2, U.S. servicemen witnessed the Japanese signing their surrender.

Japanese prisoners of war in Guam bowed their heads in August 1945, after hearing that Emperor Hirohito had announced Japan's unconditional surrender.

Generals Douglas MacArthur and Jonathan Wainwright watched as the surrender documents were officially signed.

A jubilant crowd of Italian-Americans waved flags and tossed papers in the air of their New York neighborhood in celebration of Japan's unconditional surrender.

Victory Over Japan Day

Japan's surrender was celebrated around the world. Thousands gathered in the streets to share their joy. In Britain, Australia, and the United States, the victory was marked with a two-day holiday.

On September 2, representatives from Great Britain, the United States, the Soviet Union, and China met on the deck of the USS *Missouri*, which was docked in Tokyo Bay, to sign documents officially ending World War II. Just after 9 a.m., Japanese Foreign Minister Mamoru Shigemitsu picked up a pen and added his signature on behalf of the Japanese government. Next, while his aides wept, General Yoshijiro Umezu signed for the Japanese armed forces. The ceremony lasted just 23 minutes, and it was broadcast by radio for millions to hear.

"It is my earnest hope and indeed the hope of all mankind that from this solemn occasion a better world shall emerge out of the blood and carnage of the past," MacArthur said.

Others inscribed their names on the document as the sun burned through the low-hanging clouds. The most devastating war in human history was over, but its implications would be felt for decades to come.

V-J Day, Times Square, New York City. Sailors and civilians alike celebrated the day.

Across the nation, streets were filled with jubilant celebrations like this one in Times Square, New York City.

American troops in Paris gathered at the Place de l'Opera to read about the surrender of Japan.

Reaction at Home

In the United States, Americans were both elated and relieved by the news of the Japanese surrender. After nearly four long years, the war was over, and their boys were coming home.

Approximately two million people, one of the largest crowds ever to gather in the history of Times Square, overtook the neighborhood, kissing, dancing, and cheering as a news ticker announced the end of the war. Confetti lined the street five inches deep. After so much pain and loss, peace had finally arrived.

9 | THE AFTERMATH

FOR THE COUNTRIES DIRECTLY AFFECTED BY THE WAR,
REBUILDING BECAME A LONG, DIFFICULT PROCESS.

In 1950, a crowd in South Korea waved a huge United Nations flag in support of Syngman Rhee, the country's first president. Rhee held strong hopes that the UN would continue to push for the unification of North and South Korea.

"The only way human beings can win a war is to prevent it."

—George C. Marshall, 1947

American troops arrested a German sniper at the end of the war. By 1945, thousands of Germans had been captured by Allied forces.

A Global Shift

AT WAR'S END, ALLIED LEADERS SHARED MANY OF THE SAME VIEWS, BUT THEY DID NOT ALWAYS HAVE THE SAME GOALS.

Following the surrender of Germany and Japan, a new world order began to emerge. Under conditions established by the Potsdam Agreement and the Potsdam Declaration, Allied victors controlled the two nations as well as the territories each country had seized during the war.

Signed on August 2, 1945, by U.S. President Harry Truman, Soviet Premier Joseph Stalin, and British Prime Minister Winston Churchill, the Potsdam Agreement would have a profound effect on the future of Germany. It not only demilitarized the country, it purged former Nazi Party members from the government and sought to remove any vestiges of Nazism from German life. The agreement divided Germany and Austria into four occupied zones and handed control of the new government to an Allied Control Council. Territorial boundaries were reestablished, and Germans living in what became Poland were removed.

The Potsdam Declaration signed on July 26 by Truman, Churchill, and Chiang Kai-shek, Chairman of the Nationalist Government of China, would have equally far-reaching consequences for Japan. In outlining the terms of surrender and what would follow, the declaration stripped Japan's military of control of the government and ordered an occupation by the Allied forces. In time, the declaration would allow the Japanese the opportunity to form a democratic government, but government control would be limited to their own home islands. Freedom of speech and religion would be established.

Other roles also shifted. The United States took its place as a superpower, and the Soviet Union moved to carve out its own sphere of influence in Europe. The end of World War II touched off a new power struggle—a Cold War that would last nearly half a century.

Peace Amid Conflict

Undercutting the calm of the postwar years in Europe and the United States was the ongoing menace of communism and Cold War power conflicts.

AUGUST 1945 Douglas MacArthur was appointed to oversee the occupation and rebuilding of Japan.

NOVEMBER 20, 1945 Nazi war criminal trials began in Nuremberg. Nearly 200 German and Austrians were tried; most were found guilty.

MAY 1946 Toyko war criminal trials, in which both military and governmental leaders faced courts run by the Allies, began.

MARCH 12, 1947 Truman addressed Congress, giving principles of the Truman Doctrine.

1945 • • • • 1945 • • • • 1946 • • • • 1947 • •

Holding English-language newspapers aloft, troops stationed in Paris celebrated Japan's surrender.

President Harry Truman (center) helped initiate the Berlin Airlift, which began in 1948 and provided tons of supplies and food to citizens living in West Berlin. Prime Minister Winston Churchill is pictured on the left, Premier Joseph Stalin on the right.

STRENGTH FOR THE FREE WORLD
FROM THE UNITED STATES OF AMERICA

MARCH 1948 Marshall Plan, providing $13 billion in relief aid, was approved.

JUNE 1948 The Soviets sealed off all railway and highway access to West Berlin, the first event of the Cold War. Western powers responded with the Berlin airlift, providing supplies and food to residents of Berlin.

APRIL 4, 1949 NATO, a military alliance of Western pro-democratic nations, was formed. Members pledged to help one another if any of them were attacked.

JUNE 1950 North Korea invaded South Korea, starting the Korean War. The conflict ended in July 1953 with an armistice between the two nations.

OCTOBER 1962 The Cuban Missile Crisis, a face-off between the Soviet Union and the United States, almost resulted in nuclear war.

General Hideki Tojo, who served as Japan's prime minister from 1941 until 1944, took the stand during his trial for war crimes.

War Crimes and the International Military Tribunals

JUSTICE WOULD BE SERVED, BUT IT WOULD NEVER MAKE UP FOR THE MILLIONS WHO LOST THEIR LIVES.

In the years following the war, hundreds of Germans and Japanese faced war crime trials.

The Nuremberg Trials

If Berlin was the heart of Nazi power during the war, Nuremberg was the center of Nazi spiritualism. The city had hosted numerous Nazi Party rallies during the 1930s and also gave birth to the Race Laws of 1935. Those regulations, also known as the Nuremberg Laws, paved the way for Hitler's Final Solution.

Given that history, it seemed fitting that accused Nazi war criminals from the political and military sectors should be prosecuted in Nuremberg, and on November 20, 1945, the trial of major war criminals began. Adolf Hitler, SS Reich Leader Heinrich Himmler, and Reich Minister of Propaganda Joseph Goebbels were already dead, having committed suicide during the final days of the war.

The International Military Tribunal, set up to try some of the most infamous war criminals in the first of the Nuremberg trials, included judges and prosecutors from the United States, Britain, France, and the Soviet Union. The 24 defendants, only 21 of whom were present at the trial, were charged with a variety of war crimes. All but three were found guilty, and 12 were sentenced to death. The others received prison sentences ranging from 10 years to life.

Ernst Kaltenbrunner, on trial here, was a feared senior member of the SS, responsible for thousands of deaths during the Holocaust. He was sentenced to death for crimes against humanity and executed in October 1946.

Nazi Reichsmarschall Hermann Göring testified at his war crime trial.

A further 12 trials known collectively as the Subsequent Nuremberg Proceedings were conducted by U.S. military tribunals between December 1946 and April 1949. In total, 185 defendants were indicted, including Nazi doctors and judges; 12 were sentenced to death, 8 were given life in prison, and some 77 others were given prison sentences of varying lengths.

Japanese War Crimes

The Potsdam Declaration specified that all those who had "deceived and misled the people of Japan into embarking on world conquest" were to be stripped of authority and influence, and that stern justice would be imposed on all war criminals. U.S. General Douglas MacArthur, who was in charge of the Japanese occupation, wasted no time in implementing this directive. The Empire of Japan surrendered on September 2, 1945, bringing the war to an end. Less than one week later, MacArthur arrested 39 people, including most of Japan's war cabinet. The Tokyo Trials began in May 1946, and high-ranking politicians and military leaders stood before prosecutors and judges. Even Tokyo Rose, Iva Toguri D'Aquino, whose propaganda-filled broadcasts had been beamed to American troops, faced prosecution.

The Tokyo War Crimes Tribunal garnered international attention, but they were not the only trials for those accused of war crimes. About 5,000 Japanese citizens were brought to trial in Japan, China, and other Asian countries. More than half of those were sentenced to life in prison, and nearly 900 were executed.

Administering Justice
Associate Supreme Court Justice Robert Jackson was selected by President Harry Truman to serve as the chief prosecutor for the International Military Tribunal. Justice Jackson later said that his work at Nuremberg was the most important of his life, as it allowed him to set legal precedents that continued to positively affect the international community.

The Most Notorious World War II Criminals

ALLIED JUDGES, PROSECUTORS, AND THEN EXECUTIONERS
ALL HAD A ROLE TO PLAY IN ADMINISTERING JUSTICE.

Japan

Iwane Matsui
Under the direction of General Iwane Matsui (1878–1948), commander of the Shanghai Expeditionary Force, Japanese troops committed a wide range of atrocities in China, including the Rape of Nanking. The Allies held Matsui responsible for the carnage and sentenced him to death. Matsui was hanged on December 23, 1948.

Akira Muto
Japanese General Akira Muto (1892–1948) served as vice chief of staff of the China Expeditionary Force during the Rape of Nanking and then as director of the Military Affairs Bureau when Pearl Harbor was bombed. Like Matsui, Muto was sentenced to death and executed on December 23, 1948.

Hideki Tojo
The prime minister of Japan at the beginning of World War II, Hideki Tojo (1884–1948) was held responsible for his government's aggressive foreign policy and for permitting the abuse of prisoners of war. He was hanged on December 23, 1948. Douglas MacArthur, who did not want to antagonize or further embarrass the Japanese people, allowed no photographs of the execution.

Germany

Hermann Göring

Hermann Göring (1893–1946), the Nazi Reichsmarschall and chief of the Luftwaffe, surrendered to American officers on May 8, 1945, and was convicted at Nuremberg. He arranged slave labor and was known to have looted art treasures from occupied territories. The day before he was to be hanged, Göring killed himself by taking a cyanide pill that was smuggled into his prison cell. In his suicide note, Göring said hanging was an inappropriate method of death for a man in his position.

Rudolf Hess

Hitler's deputy Rudolf Hess (1894–1987) was a devout Nazi who signed decrees authorizing the persecution of Jews. His loyalty was rewarded in 1933, when Hitler named Hess second in the line of succession, following Göring. Hess was sentenced to life in prison and committed suicide in 1987 at the age of 93.

Fritz Sauckel

Hitler's chief of slave labor recruiting, Fritz Sauckel (1894–1946) was responsible for finding workers in Nazi-occupied territories. Under Sauckel's leadership, five million people were deported to serve as slave labor and subjected to cruel, ruthless working conditions. He was executed on October 16, 1946.

Martin Bormann

Hitler's personal secretary, Martin Bormann (1900–1945), was also head of the Party Chancellery. His influence over Hitler was so strong, some have said he was the secret leader of the Nazis. When it came time for trial in Nuremberg, Bormann could not be found. His counsel argued that he was dead, but there was no proof. Bormann was tried in absentia and sentenced to death by hanging. He was formally pronounced dead in 1973, but his true fate remains a mystery.

Julius Streicher

Julius Streicher (1885–1946), an anti-Semitic newspaper editor, earned the moniker "the number one Jew-baiter" during Nazi rule. He organized a boycott of Jewish businesses in 1933, publicly supported the Nuremberg Laws, and called for the total destruction of the Jewish race. Streicher was sentenced to death at Nuremberg and was hanged on October 16, 1946.

An American serviceman shared his rations with hungry children in Okinawa in the summer of 1945.

Transforming Japan

AS U.S. AND BRITISH PERSONNEL ARRIVED TO OCCUPY THE ISLAND NATION, NEW POLITICAL AND SOCIAL INSTITUTIONS WERE CREATED.

In September 1945, Gen. Douglas MacArthur, with the title of the Supreme Commander for the Allied Powers, took charge of the occupation of Japan. Although the principles and plans for the occupation had been developed in Washington, DC, it was MacArthur, who within just five-and-a-half years, helped transform the country and remake its society into one of the world's leading democracies.

The makeover unfolded with amazing speed and efficiency. In April 1946, the Japanese held democratic elections. The government established civil rights, allowed labor to unionize, took initial steps to establish equal rights for women, instituted land reform, stripped the emperor of divine status, and created a constitution that outlawed war and guarded against remilitarization. As part of the American reconstruction policy, MacArthur allowed Emperor Hirohito to retain the throne in order to "maintain a completely orderly government." The emperor backed the constitution.

American combat engineers helped rebuild Okinawa. Here they worked to restore a bridge.

Food-filled boxes labeled "These canned goods are American presents. Let us thank the United States," in both Japanese and English, were distributed to hungry Japanese.

General Douglas MacArthur worked with Japanese Emperor Hirohito to ensure a smooth postwar transition for Japan. This photo was taken in 1945, at the U.S. Embassy in Tokyo.

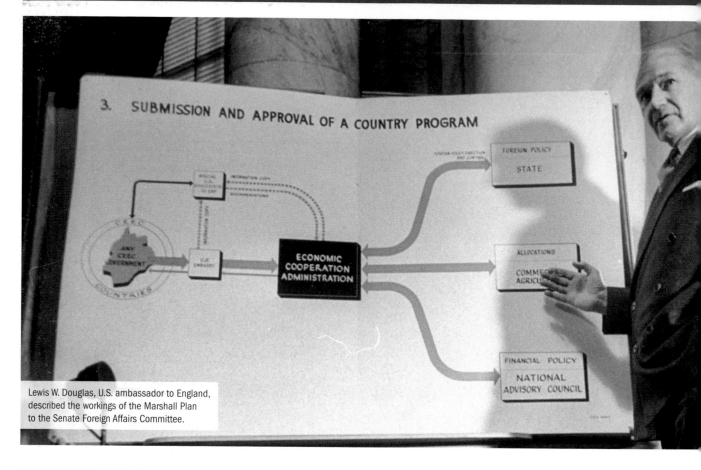

Lewis W. Douglas, U.S. ambassador to England, described the workings of the Marshall Plan to the Senate Foreign Affairs Committee.

George C. Marshall

George C. Marshall (1880–1959) was a career military officer who served as chief of staff, with the rank of general, during the war. From 1947 to 1949, Marshall served as secretary of state, and it was during this time that he formulated the Marshall Plan. Marshall believed that his plan would jumpstart European industrialization. It would also stimulate the American economy by establishing new overseas markets for American products. Marshall was awarded the Nobel Peace Prize in 1953.

Billions in Aid to Rebuild Europe

TO BATTLE THE GROWING INFLUENCE OF THE SOVIETS, GEORGE MARSHALL PROPOSED AN AMBITIOUS PLAN.

Europe had been devastated by World War II. Industrial areas, residential neighborhoods, and once-thriving farmland lay in ruins. In some regions, the civilian populations were starving to death. Many economies were on the brink of collapse. There were few jobs. Trains did not run; roads were impassable.

In Germany, the war had destroyed 25 percent of all urban housing, while the country's gross domestic product had fallen 70 percent. Food production dropped dramatically, and industrial output was just one-third of its prewar level. British and American policy makers feared that if the United States did not take an active role in rebuilding Western Europe, the dire conditions could possibly open the door to further Communist influence.

In the spring of 1947, Secretary of State George C. Marshall proposed an audacious plan: that the United States send billions of dollars in aid to rescue the shattered economies. Congress approved the concept and in March 1948 passed the Economic Cooperation Act—the Marshall Plan— earmarking $12 billion for the effort.

Eventually 16 governments participated in the Marshall Plan and accepted nearly $13 billion in aid. Stalin, however, barred Eastern European countries from participating. Instead, he promised these countries help from the Soviet Union. Division lines between East and West once again were being drawn and reinforced.

American and British dignitaries gathered at the Royal Victoria Dock in London to herald the first shipment of sugar sent as part of the Marshall Plan.

Homes, businesses, and houses of worship all had to be rebuilt. The town of Caen in Normandy was particularly hard hit; rebuilding was not completed until 1962.

DECLARATION BY UNITED NATIONS

In 1942, delegates from 26 nations joined together to sign the UN Declaration, binding these countries together against the Axis powers.

The United Nations Becomes a Reality

PRESIDENT FRANKLIN ROOSEVELT'S VISION OF AN INTERNATIONAL PEACEKEEPING ORGANIZATION TOOK ITS PLACE ON THE INTERNATIONAL STAGE.

Born from the desire to mediate international disputes and to maintain peace around the world, the United Nations was officially formed in 1945.

It was not the first time that world leaders had attempted to create such an organization. At the end of World War I, President Woodrow Wilson had proposed a similar idea and was able to enlist 48 countries to join the League of Nations to settle disputes within Europe. However, member nations could not use force to settle problems. When the organization failed to prevent the outbreak of World War II, it was disbanded.

Founders of the United Nations were determined to avoid that fate and began establishing and agreeing upon principles as early as 1941. The primary goal of the member nations was to support one another through the war and to establish a foundation for peace in the postwar future.

On January 1, 1942, leaders of the United States, Great Britain, the Soviet Union, and China, as well as delegates from 26 Allied nations, met in Washington, DC, and signed the Declaration of the United Nations.

Over the next three years, more nations were invited to join, and ultimately delegates and staff from 50 nations came together to create a charter for the new organization. In this document, delegates laid out the foundation for the United Nations, whose job it would be, among other things, to "save succeeding generations from the scourge of war . . . to reaffirm faith in fundamental human rights . . ." The UN Charter called for nations to respect equal rights and the self-determination of all peoples. It also set up a Security Council, which would be given significant authority and means to maintain peace. This authority included applying economic sanctions and sending peacekeeping forces to help resolve disputes among nations. The Security Council had five permanent members—the United States, Great Britain, France, the Soviet Union, and China—and each nation would have veto power on any council decision.

The UN was soon called into action and its powers tested. In May 1948, the organization called for an end to the battles in Palestine. Since that time, UN peacekeeping forces have remained in the Middle East monitoring cease-fires and armistice agreements. In June 1950, member nations were called to help South Korea repel North Korea's advances. The Security Council, without participation from the Soviet Union, voted to send troops to South Korea, pushing the Cold War into Asia.

The first UN sessions in April 1945 were held at the San Francisco Opera House (shown here) and at the Veterans Building. More than 3,500 delegates and staff members participated.

In October 1949, officials held the UN flag in front of the unfinished building in New York City; in 1950, the Secretariat building opened; the entire complex was finished in 1952.

Delegates to the UN meetings held in San Francisco came from the United States, France, Britain, Russia, and China.

Truman signed the Atomic Energy Act of 1946, establishing the U.S. Atomic Energy Commission and putting nuclear weapons and nuclear power development under civilian control.

In March 1947, Truman announced his new foreign policy at a joint session of Congress.

George F. Kennan

Just after the war, American diplomat George Kennan, U.S. chargé d'affaires in Moscow, wrote a document known as the "Long Telegram," in which he described the aggressiveness of Soviet policy and suggested that it was unlikely there would be any long-term accords between the United States and the Soviet Union. Americans, Kennan wrote, should be prepared for a patient, vigilant containment of the Russian "expansive tendencies." Laying out what would become U.S. policy, he said the best defense was to prevent the spread of communism.

America's New Role

TRUMAN DREW A LINE IN THE SAND TO KEEP DEMOCRATIC NATIONS FREE FROM COMMUNIST INFLUENCE.

Before his death in 1945, Franklin D. Roosevelt tried to ensure that the peace achieved at the end of World War II would endure by keeping intact the alliance between Great Britain, the United States, and the Soviet Union. But it became clear at Potsdam that the cooperation among the "Big Three" would not last long after the Axis powers surrendered.

Roosevelt's approach failed because the dynamics of world power had shifted from six great nations to just two—the United States and the Soviet Union. In 1947, the Communists threatened to destabilize the pro-Western governments of Greece

and Turkey. Truman, who had become president upon Roosevelt's death, urged Congress to support both countries.

The Truman Doctrine

On March 2, 1947, Truman addressed Congress with the outlines of a new strategy to contain Soviet expansion. The United States, he explained, would politically, militarily, and economically assist all democratic nations under threat from inside or outside authoritarian forces. This proposal, called the Truman Doctrine, would guide American foreign policy for decades and allowed the United States to intervene in faraway conflicts, even though those conflicts might not directly involve America.

NATO and the Warsaw Pact

Two new major military alliances followed the Truman Doctrine. In 1949, the United States and 11 other Western nations formed NATO,

When President Truman addressed the joint session of Congress, he was met with a standing ovation.

U.S. Secretary of Defense Louis Johnson addressed a meeting of NATO delegates in April 1950. They approved the plan to protect their countries from outside aggression.

the North Atlantic Treaty Organization. The goal of this organization was to come to the defense of any member nations attacked by enemy countries. Germany, which was re-arming itself, joined NATO on May 9, 1955. The Soviet Union saw its old enemy on its eastern border, and less than one week later, on May 14, the Soviet Union, along with seven satellite nations, established the Warsaw Pact, a military alliance with the same mission as NATO—to protect member nations against attack. Europe was now aligned into two camps, providing the framework for the military standoff of the Cold War.

The Cold War

English writer George Orwell coined the term "Cold War" in 1945 in reference to life under the threat of nuclear war. The phrase soon came to be associated with the sustained political and military tensions that existed between the Western and Eastern Bloc nations, particularly the U.S. and the Soviet Union. In the United States, the Cold War resulted in an unprecedented buildup of arms. With the Truman Doctrine and the creation of NATO and the Warsaw Pact, the Cold War would last until the 1990s.

NATO

While NATO's primary purpose was to respond to threats posed by the Soviet Union, the alliance was designed to deter Soviet expansionism, stop nationalist militarism in Europe, and encourage political integration of Europe.

An Iron Curtain Descends Across Europe

ONCE AGAIN, THE WORLD WAS DIVIDED AS
COMMUNISM SPREAD INTO NEW TERRITORIES.

On March 5, 1946, Churchill, who had recently been voted out of office as Britain's prime minister, traveled to Westminster College in Missouri. An ardent anti-Communist, Churchill gave a blistering speech warning against Soviet designs in Europe. "From Stettin in the Baltic to Trieste in the Adriatic, an Iron Curtain has descended across the Continent," Churchill declared. The phrase "Iron Curtain" shook the West to its core, changing the way it looked at the Communist threat.

Fascism had been annihilated, but communism remained a menace to the Western democracies. After World War II, the Soviet Union became the dominant force in Eastern Europe. The Soviets, who had suffered greatly at the hands of the Nazis, wanted to establish a defensive zone on their western border, and they intended to establish a Communist government in Poland.

Under Stalin, the Soviets continued to bring countries that the Red Army had liberated from the Nazis, including Poland, Hungary, Albania, and Bulgaria among others, under Communist control by working with local Communists and helping to indoctrinate the people of Eastern Europe with the message that socialism was far superior to capitalism. The Communists set up secret police forces, arrested political opponents, and took control of the military in these countries.

By 1949, all Eastern European governments except Yugoslavia had become Soviet puppet states. That same year, Germany, which had been divided into four zones, also underwent major changes. The areas occupied by the United States, France, and Great Britain were combined to form the Federal Republic of Germany, or West Germany. The zone under Soviet control became the German Democratic Republic, or East Germany, where a Communist society was put in place. These moves divided Europe geographically into the Western Bloc and the Eastern Bloc, each of which had very different ideas about government.

In September 1949, Americans were shocked when they heard that the Soviets had detonated their first atomic bomb a month earlier, proving that the Communist threat had the potential to hit much closer to home than many had expected.

Communists in Asia
In 1949, Cold War tensions also shifted to the Far East when the Communists, led by Mao Zedong, captured Beijing and took over China, ousting the Chinese Nationalists. President Harry Truman faced harsh criticism from those who thought he had "lost" China to communism, and critics blamed him for not providing enough aid to the Chinese Nationalists.

In his famous "Iron Curtain" speech, Churchill praised the United States and discussed the need for continuing close relations between the U.S. and Great Britain.

East German soldiers standing guard at the Berlin Wall, which finally fell in 1989.

American soldiers were joined by troops from 15 other UN member nations, joining together to thwart advances by North Korea.

UN troops successfully landed at Incheon, South Korea, on September 15, 1950. They cut North Korea's army in half and pushed their forces back to the north.

New Battlefields Abroad and at Home

THE COLD WAR HEATED UP IN THE FIRST MILITARY
CONFRONTATION BETWEEN COMMUNISM AND DEMOCRACY.

The first major test of the Truman Doctrine and the United Nations occurred in 1950 when North Korea invaded South Korea.

North Korean leader Kim Il-Sung, hoping to reunite the North and South and form a single Communist state, spent months planning an invasion and looked to Stalin for support. At first, the Soviet leader was reluctant, knowing such actions might incite a war with the United States. But after the USSR tested its first atomic bomb, Stalin felt more secure and agreed to back Kim.

Truman asked the United Nations to help stop the assault. When the North Koreans refused to honor the UN order to halt the invasion, the organization sent military forces, led by the United States, to assist South Korea.

The Korean War ended in a stalemate in 1953, and while an armistice was signed, no peace treaty was ever negotiated. Approximately 54,000 Americans died fighting in the conflict, and it fundamentally changed America's military role in the world. Until then, U.S. foreign policy had relied on economic assistance to other countries to stem the Communist threat. Korea was a sharp departure from that strategy, as the U.S. put the Communist world on notice that it would resort to military force if necessary. The decision would prove costly to the United States in the 1960s and 1970s during the Vietnam War.

Red Scare at Home

As the Cold War shifted into high gear, opportunists looked for real and perceived Communists in the U.S. Using smear and slander, "Red baiting," or accusing or persecuting a person or group as Communist, became popular. U.S. Senator Joseph McCarthy rose to fame in 1950 when he announced that he had evidence of a spy ring in the State Department. Over the next few years, more than 1,700 federal employees suspected of Communist sympathies were dismissed, while another 1,200 or so resigned. The military discharged more than 2,200 servicemen and -women. Finally, following a government hearing in June 1954, the Senate condemned McCarthy's conduct.

U.S. troops became heavily involved in the Vietnam War. The first U.S. ground troops were sent in 1965; the last left in 1973.

Known for his staunch anti-Communist stance, Senator Joseph McCarthy, shown here at a 1954 Army-McCarthy hearing, was first elected to the U.S. Senate in 1946.

Servicemen returning home took advantage of the G.I. Bill and returned to school.

The Postwar Years in the United States

WHILE EUROPEANS TRIED TO RECOVER FROM THE WAR, AMERICANS PROSPERED.

Though it took nearly two years to restore Pearl Harbor and the ships that had been damaged there, the United States did not suffer from the major destruction that affected its allies and foes in Europe. As weary veterans returned home to peace, they were ready to move on with their lives.

Boom Times

The postwar years in the United States were marked by political stability and economic prosperity. Although there were periods of inflation, loss of defense jobs, and the challenge of thousands of soldiers returning to civilian life, the nation was on the rise and the economy boomed. As President Truman remarked, by the end of 1946, less than a year-and-a-half after V-J Day, millions of demobilized veterans and wartime workers had found employment in one of the largest changeovers that any nation had ever experienced as it went from war to peace.

Defense contractors began retooling their plants and factories to produce the goods that consumers now craved. War rationing was over, most people were finding jobs, and finally, cars, refrigerators, TVs, and even homes were all for sale in mass quantities.

Appliances, televisions, even vacuum cleaners became available to consumers.

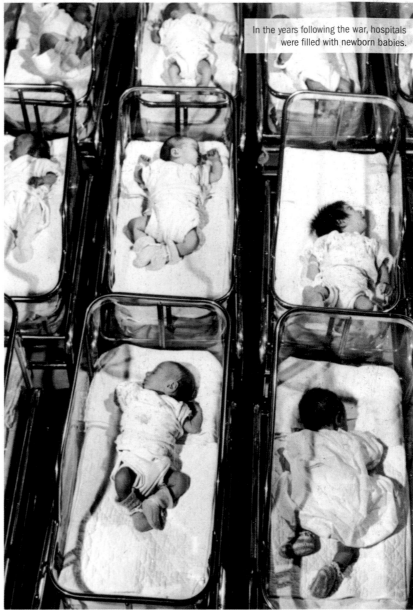

In the years following the war, hospitals were filled with newborn babies.

The G.I. Bill

Near the war's end, Congress and President Roosevelt discussed ways to ease the transition of returning soldiers by assisting them financially. One of the results was the Servicemen's Readjustment Act of 1944, also known as the G.I. Bill, signed into law on June 22, 1944. As part of the subsidies tied to the bill, the government guaranteed home and business loans, making it possible for veterans to buy their own houses and start businesses. The bill also included subsidies for education, and by the mid-1950s, more than two million vets had used their benefits to attend college, high school, and vocational school.

Oh, Baby!

Returning veterans were eager to marry and start families, which resulted in a "baby boom" that changed the makeup of the country. In the 1950s, the population grew by almost 30 million, and between 1940 and 1957, the birth rate rose nearly one-third. This population spurt triggered economic development, as demand rose for new homes, new schools, and new consumer goods. It had another major effect: the spread of suburbs throughout the nation. By 1950, a critical housing shortage ended when large numbers of mass-produced homes hit the market.

Thousands gathered in Berlin on the night of November 9, 1989, to celebrate the fall of the Berlin Wall.

Vanquished No More

GERMANY AND JAPAN, TORN AND BELEAGUERED IN 1945
WERE BOTH ABLE TO TURN THEIR ECONOMIES AROUND.

West Germany Rebuilds

Bolstered by Marshall Plan loans of about $1.5 billion (about $15 billion today), West Germany made a remarkable comeback following the war.

In 1948, the country introduced a social market economy that combined aspects of traditional capitalism and more liberal social policies. This new model allowed West Germany to rebuild itself physically and led to an economic boom that turned West Germany into one of the richest nations in the world.

The collapse of communism in 1989 brought other major changes, including the demolition of the Berlin Wall, which had cut off West Berlin from both East Berlin and East Germany since 1961. The fall of the wall paved the way for the reunification of East and West Germany, and on October 3, 1990, the two countries reunited into the Federal Republic of Germany. Some believe that October 3, 1990, represents the end of the Cold War.

Tokyo, a bustling, modern city, has recovered from the war's devastation.

Today, Germany is a strong democracy and has one of the world's largest economies. It joined the UN in 1973 and is a leader in the European Union. Its population has rebounded, too, and it now has the biggest population of any European Union country.

Japan Vaults Ahead

In 1950, Japan was still occupied by American forces, but reforms affecting nearly every aspect of daily life had been instituted, and the economy and political future of the island nation was secure. Soon, Japan would be free from occupation.

In 1951, the country signed a security pact allowing the United States to keep its military bases on Okinawa and by 1952, American military occupation forces had been removed.

Since that time, Japan has thrived beyond all expectations. It has become an economic leader and industrial force with factories that export everything from trains and streetcars to medical equipment to computers. The country has dominated the automobile business, increasing vehicle exports from 10,000 in 1961 to one million in the early 1970s. By 2008, Toyota was the world's No. 1 carmaker, a title it held until 2011. The country's population has recovered from the losses sustained during the war, and in terms of education, Japan has excelled as well. Its students continually rank high in international standards.

INDEX

PHOTO CREDITS

Bottom: Hulton Archive/Getty Images p. 132: Keystone/Hulton Archive/Getty Images p. 133: Top: Popperfoto/Getty Images p. 133: Top: © CORBIS p. 134: Top: Paul Popper/Popperfoto/Getty Images p. 135: Top: Haynes Archive/Popperfoto/Getty Images p. 135: Bottom Left: MPI/Getty Images p. 135: Bottom Right: Capt. G Keating/IWM/Getty Images pp. 136–137: ASSOCIATED PRESS

6: THE TIDE OF WAR TURNS

pp. 138–139: Popperfoto/Getty Images p. 140: Top Left: Keystone/Hulton Archive/Getty Images pp. 140–141: Frank Scherschel/Time Life Pictures/Getty Images p. 141: Right row: Top to Bottom: National Archives/Photo Researchers/Getty Images; Keystone/Hulton Archive/Getty Images; Fox Photos/Hulton Archive/Getty Images pp. 142–143: US Marine Corps/Interim Archives/Getty Images p. 143: Top: Hulton Archive/Getty Images p. 143: Bottom Left: Lawrence Thornton/Archive Photos/Getty Images p. 143: Bottom Right: Fotosearch/Getty Images pp. 144–145: Top Left: Tim Graham/Fox Photos/Hulton Archive/Getty Images pp. 144–145: Bottom Center: Stanley Sherman/London Express/Hulton Archive/Getty Images p. 145: Right: © The Art Archive/Alamy p. 146: Top: Manchester Daily Express/SSPL/Getty Images p. 146: Bottom: Galerie Bilderwelt/Hulton Archive/Getty Images p. 147: Top: Unidentified Author/Alinari Archives, Florence/Alinari via Getty Images p. 147: Bottom: Roger Viollet/Getty Images p. 148: Top Left: Popperfoto/Getty Images p. 148: Bottom Left: Popperfoto/Getty Images p. 148: Bottom Right: Popperfoto/Getty Images pp. 148–149: Hulton Archive/Getty Images p. 150: Top: U.S. Army Air Force/ASSOCIATED PRESS p. 150: Bottom: Hulton Archive/Getty Images p. 151: Top: Photo12/UIG/Getty Images p. 151: Bottom: Popperfoto/Getty Images p. 152: Fox Photos/Hulton Archive/Getty Images p. 153: Top: Galerie Bilderwelt/Hulton Archive/Getty Images p. 153: Bottom: © INTERFOTO/Alamy pp. 154–155: Pictorial Parade/Archive Photos/Getty Images p. 155: Top: Keystone/Hulton Archive/Getty Images p. 155: Bottom: Hulton Archive/Getty Images p. 156: Top: Universal History Archive/UIG/Getty Images p. 157: LAPI/Roger Viollet/Getty Images p. 158: Hulton Archive/Getty Images p. 159: Top: Hart Preston/Time & Life Pictures/Getty Images p. 159: Center: SSPL/Getty Images p. 160: Popperfoto/Getty Images p. 161: Top: Royal Air Force Official Photographer/IWM/Getty Images p. 161: Bottom Left: Popperfoto/Getty Images p. 161: Bottom Right: Keystone/Hulton Archive/Getty Images p. 162: Left: PhotoQuest/Getty Images pp. 162–163: Lt. C H Parnall/IWM/Getty Images p. 163: Top Left: Keystone/Hulton Archive/Getty Images p. 163: Bottom: Mondadori Portfolio/Getty Images p. 164: Top: Sovfoto/UIG/Getty Images p. 165: Top: Mondadori Portfolio/Getty Images pp. 164–165: Bottom: Sovfoto/UIG/Getty Images p. 166: Left: Keystone/Hulton Archive/Getty Images p. 166: Top: Roger Viollet/Getty Images p. 167: Top: Sovfoto/UIG/Getty Images p. 167: Bottom: Sovfoto/UIG/Getty Images pp. 168–169: Top Center: Sovfoto/UIG/Getty Images pp. 168–169: Bottom Center: Mondadori Portfolio/Getty Images p. 169: Keystone-France/Gamma-Keystone/Getty Images p. 170: Top: Hulton Archive/Getty Images pp. 170–171: PhotoQuest/Getty Images p. 172: Underwood Archives/Getty Images p. 173: Top: Keystone/Hulton Archive/Getty Images p. 173: Paul Popper/Popperfoto/Getty Images

7: OVERWHELMING FORCE

pp. 174–175: Robert F Sargent/Getty Images pp. 176–177: Top: Popperfoto/Getty Images p. 176: Center: Daily Herald Archive/SSPL/Getty Images p. 177: Sovfoto/UIG/Getty Images pp. 176–177: Bottom Row: Left to Right: STF/AFP/Getty Images; Galerie Bilderwelt/Hulton Archive/Getty Images; Galerie Bilderwelt/Hulton Archive/Getty Images; © Hulton-Deutsch Collection/CORBIS; © Bettmann/CORBIS; ASSOCIATED PRESS; Photo12/UIG/Getty Images; pp. 178–179: Top: Sovfoto/UIG/Getty Images p. 178: Bottom Left: Sovfoto/UIG/Getty Images p. 179: Bottom: Sovfoto/UIG via Getty Images p. 180: Keystone/Hulton Archive/Getty Images p. 181: Top Left: BRITISH OFFICIAL PHOTO/AP p. 181: Top Center: Popperfoto/Getty Images p. 181: Top Right: Paul Popper/Popperfoto/Getty Images p. 181: © Steve Kaufman/CORBIS p. 182: Bottom: Galerie Bilderwelt/Hulton Archive/Getty Images p. 183: Top: Keystone/Hulton Archive/Getty Images p. 183 Bottom: Nat Farbman/Time Life Pictures/Getty Images p. 184: Berliner Verlag/Archiv/picture-alliance/dpa/AP Images pp. 184–185: Center Top: Galerie Bilderwelt/Hulton Archive/Getty Images p. 185: FPG/Getty Images pp. 184–185: Bottom: Camerique/Getty Images p. 186: Left: David E. Scherman/Time Life Pictures/Getty Images p. 186: Right: Galerie Bilderwelt/Hulton Archive/Getty Images p. 187: Galerie Bilderwelt/Hulton Archive/Getty Images p. 188: Top Left: MPI/Getty Images p. 188: Top Right: Capt. E G Malindine/IWM/Getty Images p. 188: Center Left: Galerie Bilderwelt/Hulton Archive/Getty Images p. 188: Center Right: Galerie Bilderwelt/Hulton Archive/Getty Images p. 188: Bottom Left: STF/AFP/Getty Images p. 188: Bottom Right: Galerie Bilderwelt/Hulton Archive/Getty Images p. 189: Top Left: US Army Air Force/US Army Air Force/Time & Life Pictures/Getty Images p. 189: Top Right: Frank Scherschel/Time Life Pictures/Getty Images p. 189: Center Left: Galerie Bilderwelt/Hulton Archive/Getty Images p. 189: Center Right: Popperfoto/Getty Images p. 189: Bottom Left: Roger Viollet/Getty Images p. 189: Bottom Right: Galerie Bilderwelt/Hulton Archive/Getty Images p. 190: Sovfoto/UIG/Getty Images p. 191: Top: Sovfoto/UIG/Getty Images p. 191: Bottom: Sovfoto/UIG/Getty Images pp. 192–193: Sovfoto/UIG/Getty Images p. 193: Center Right: Hulton Archive/Getty Images p. 193: Bottom: Sovfoto/UIG/Getty Images p. 194: Top: US Signal Corps/Time & Life Pictures/Getty Images p. 194: Bottom Left: Fred Ramage/Keystone/Getty Images p. 194: Bottom Right: MPI/Getty Images p. 195: Keystone/Hulton Archive/Getty Images p. 196: Left: © CORBIS pp. 196–197: Top: © CORBIS pp. 196–197: Bottom Left: Roger Viollet/Getty Images p. 197: Bottom Right: ASSOCIATED PRESS p. 198: © The Art Archive/Alamy p. 199: Top: Time Life Pictures/US Navy/National Archives/Time Life Pictures/Getty Images p. 199: Bottom: Keystone/Hulton Archive/Getty Images p. 200: © CORBIS p. 201: Top Left: ASSOCIATED PRESS p. 201: Top Right: Galerie Bilderwelt/Hulton Archive/Getty Images p. 201: Bottom: © CORBIS p. 202: Bottom: US Army/Time & Life Pictures/Getty Images pp. 202–203: © INTERFOTO/Alamy pp. 204–205: 1: © dk/Alamy; 2: © INTERFOTO/Alamy; 3: © INTERFOTO/Alamy; 4: © Richard Allen/Alamy; 5: © Stocktrek Images, Inc./Alamy; 6: © Chris Howes/Wild Places Photography/Alamy; 7: © INTERFOTO/Alamy; 8: Gary Ombler/Dorling Kindersley/Getty Images; 9: © Jeffrey Jones/Alamy; 10: © INTERFOTO/Alamy; 11: © INTERFOTO/Alamy; 12: Jean-Louis Dubois

8: THE END OF THE WAR

pp. 206–207: Popperfoto/Getty Images p. 208: Sovfoto/UIG/Getty Images p. 209: Left: Universal History Archive/Getty Images p. 209: Right row: Top to Bottom: ASSOCIATED PRESS; Keystone/Hulton Archive/Getty Images; Kallista Images/Getty Images pp. 210–211: Top: Keystone/Hulton Archive/Getty Images p. 211: Top: War Office Official Photographer/IWM/Getty Images pp. 210–211: Bottom: George Skadding/Time Life Pictures/Getty Images p. 212: Top Left: Mondadori Portfolio/Getty Images pp. 212–213: Top Center: W. Eugene Smith/Time Life Pictures/Getty Images p. 213: Top Right: JOE ROSENTHAL/ASSOCIATED PRESS p. 213: Bottom: Popperfoto/Getty Images p. 214: Top Left: ASSOCIATED PRESS p. 214: Center Left: Keystone/Hulton Archive/Getty Images pp. 214–215: © CORBIS p. 216: Top: MPI/Getty Images p. 216: Bottom: Family of Tak Kyung-hyun/ASSOCIATED PRESS p. 217: Top Left: US Navy/Time & Life Pictures/Getty Images p. 217: Top Right: © Bettmann/CORBIS p. 217: Bottom: Popperfoto/Getty Images p. 218: Top: Sovfoto/UIG/Getty Images p. 218: Center Left: Culture Club/Hulton Archive/Getty Images p. 219: Bottom Left: Sovfoto/UIG/Getty Images p. 219: Bottom Right: Sgt. Hewitt/IWM/Getty Images p. 220: Left: Galerie Bilderwelt/Hulton Archive/Getty Images pp. 220–221: Center: Horace Abrahams/Keystone/Getty Images p. 221: Right: David E. Scherman/Time & Life Pictures/Getty Images pp. 222–223: Top: PhotoQuest/Getty Images; Bottom: Gavin Whitelaw Collection/Hulton Archive/Getty Images p. 223: Top Right: ASSOCIATED PRESS p. 223: Bottom Right: Picture Post/Hulton Archive/Getty Images p. 224: Bottom Left: © CORBIS pp. 224–225: Los Alamos National Laboratory/Time & Life Pictures/Getty Images p. 225: Top: Keystone-France/Gamma-Keystone/Getty Images p. 225: Bottom: ASSOCIATED PRESS pp. 226–227: Top: SCIENCE SOURCE/Photo Researchers/Getty Images p. 227: Bottom Left: Fritz Goro/Time Life Pictures/Getty Images p. 227: Right: © CORBIS p. 228: Left: PhotoQuest/Getty Images pp. 228–229: PhotoQuest/Getty Images pp. 230–231: Top: ASSOCIATED PRESS p. 230: Bottom Left: Keystone/Hulton Archive/Getty Images pp. 230–231: Bottom Center: © CORBIS p. 231: Bottom Right: PhotoQuest/Getty Images p. 232: Bottom Left: Keystone-France/Gamma-Keystone/Getty Images pp. 232–233: © Hulton-Deutsch Collection/CORBIS p. 234: Left: © SuperStock/Corbis p. 234: Right: © Bettmann/CORBIS p. 235: Top: Popperfoto/Getty Images p. 235: Bottom: Universal/IndiaPicture p. 236: Keystone-France/Gamma-Keystone/Getty Images p. 237: Top: Hiromiti Matuda/Handout from Nagasaki Atomic Bomb Museum/Getty Images p. 237: Bottom: © Bettmann/CORBIS pp. 238–239: Abbie Rowe/PhotoQuest/Getty Images p. 238: Bottom: MPI/Getty Images p. 239: Top: © CORBIS p. 239: Bottom: ASSOCIATED PRESS p. 240: ASSOCIATED PRESS p. 241: Top Left: Alfred Eisenstaedt/Time & Life Pictures/Getty Images p. 241: Top Right: U.S. Army/ASSOCIATED PRESS p. 241: Bottom: Keystone-France/Gamma-Keystone via Getty Images

9: THE AFTERMATH

pp. 242–243: Interim Archives/Getty Images p. 244: Top: Keystone/Hulton Archive/Getty Images p. 245: Top: Photo12/UIG/Getty Images p. 245: Center: Popperfoto/Getty Images pp. 244–245: Bottom row, left to right: PhotoQuest/Getty Images; Raymond D'Addario/Galerie Bilderwelt/Hulton Archive/Getty Images; Alfred Eisenstaedt/Time & Life Pictures/Getty Images; James Whitmore/Time Life Pictures/Getty Images; Keystone-France/Gamma-Keystone/Getty Images; Henry Grant Compton/FPG/Getty Images; AFP/Getty Images; MPI/Hulton Archive/Getty Images; Carl Mydans/Time & Life Pictures/Getty Images p. 246: Top Left: AFP/Getty Images pp. 246–247: Top Center: Raymond D'Addario/Galerie Bilderwelt/Hulton Archive/Getty Images p. 247: Top Right: Kurt Hutton/Picture Post/Getty Images p. 247: Bottom: Photo12/UIG/Getty Images p. 248: Top Left: Carl Mydans/Time Life Pictures/Getty Images p. 248: Top Right: Carl Mydans/Time Life Pictures/Getty Images p. 248: Bottom: Carl Mydans/Time Life Pictures/Getty Images p. 249: Top Left: Raymond D'Addario/Galerie Bilderwelt/Hulton Archive/Getty Images p. 249: Top Right: Keystone/Hulton Archive/Getty Images p. 249: Center Left: Universal History Archive/UIG/Getty Images p. 249: Center Right: Hugo Jaeger/Timepix/Time Life Pictures/Getty Images p. 249: Bottom: Universal History Archive/Getty Images p. 250: FPG/Hulton Archive/Getty Images p. 251: Top: J.R. Eyerman/Time & Life Pictures/Getty Images; Bottom Left: © Bettmann/CORBIS; Bottom Right: JIJI PRESS/AFP/GettyImages pp. 252–253: Top Left: Francis Miller/Time Life Pictures/Getty Images p. 252: Bottom: PhotoQuest/Getty Images p. 253: Right: Edward Miller/Keystone/Getty Images pp. 252–253: Bottom: James Jarche/Popperfoto/Getty Images p. 254: Top Left: Hulton Archive/Getty Images pp. 254–255: Keystone-France/Gamma-Keystone/Getty Images p. 255: Top Right: Keystone/Hulton Archive/Getty Images; Bottom: Fox Photos/Hulton Archive/Getty Images p. 256: Left: Marie Hansen/Time Life Pictures/Getty Images; Right: Al Fenn/Time Life Pictures/Getty Images; Bottom: ASSOCIATED PRESS p. 257: Top: Al Fenn/Time Life Pictures/Getty Images; Center: Keystone/Hulton Archive/Getty Images; Bottom: Caspar Benson/Getty Images p. 258: Left: AFP/Getty Images p. 259: Top: George Skadding/Time Life Pictures/Getty Images; Bottom: GUNTHER KERN/AFP/Getty Images p. 260: Top Left: Romanowski Strickland/US Army/Time Life Pictures/Getty Images pp. 260–261: Top Center: Photo12/UIG/Getty Images p. 261: Top Right: Dick Swanson/Time & Life Pictures/Getty Images; Bottom: Hank Walker/Time Life Pictures/Getty Images p. 262: Top Left: Keystone-France/Gamma-Keystone/Getty Images pp. 262–263: Top Center: Al Moldvay/The Denver Post/Getty Images p. 263: Top Right: Three Lions/Hulton Archive/Getty Images p. 264: © Robert Wallis/SIPA/Corbis p. 265: Sandro Bisaro/Getty Images

Maps Created by Contentra Technologies: 13; 29; 53; 54; 75; 76; 125; 127; 129; 132; 156; 159; 165; 178; 192; 200; 219